Slow Down, I'm Getting Well Too Fast

Emotional Transformation Therapy (ETT)

DR. IREN FELLEGVARI

SLOW DOWN, I'M GETTING WELL TOO FAST
EMOTIONAL TRANSFORMATION THERAPY (ETT)

The information, ideas, and suggestions in this book are not intended
as a substitute for professional medical advice. Before following any
suggestions contained in this book, you should consult your personal
physician. Neither the author nor the publisher shall be liable or responsible
for any loss or damage allegedly arising as a consequence of your use
or application of any information or suggestions in this book.

iUniverse books may be ordered through booksellers or by contacting:

iUniverse LLC
1663 Liberty Drive
Bloomington, IN 47403
www.iuniverse.com
1-800-Authors (1-800-288-4677)

Because of the dynamic nature of the Internet, any web addresses or
links contained in this book may have changed since publication and
may no longer be valid. The views expressed in this work are solely those
of the author and do not necessarily reflect the views of the publisher,
and the publisher hereby disclaims any responsibility for them.

Any people depicted in stock imagery provided by Thinkstock are models,
and such images are being used for illustrative purposes only.
Certain stock imagery © Thinkstock.

ISBN: 978-1-4917-4881-7 (sc)
ISBN: 978-1-4917-4880-0 (e)
Library of Congress Control Number: 2014917494

Printed in the United States of America.

iUniverse rev. date: 09/29/2014

CONTENTS

AUTHOR'S NOTE ON GENDER IN EXAMPLES

For purposes of simplicity but not exclusion, parents and caregivers will often be referred to as "the mother" or in the feminine, and children will often be referred to as "the child" or in the masculine, to easily distinguish between caregivers and children in our discussion of attachment styles.

In the same way, for purposes of simplicity but not exclusion, therapists will often be referred to in the feminine and clients will often be referred to in the masculine, so that their roles can be distinguished during discussions in the text.

The reader should feel free to change genders and reverse male/female and female/male as desired.

INTRODUCTION

Why write this book?

I have been a therapist for about thirteen years, treating several clients a day. I have been using "traditional" psychological methods based on my clients' problems and comfort levels. I love what I am doing. Clients send me their friends and relatives. I think they're satisfied with the outcome of our work.

I try to remain up-to-date with all the new developments in my profession. When I heard for example how well Eye Movement Desensitization Reprocessing (EMDR) works with certain issues, such as trauma and PTSD, I wanted to learn it right away. With EMDR, I have been able to help many clients who had life-damaging childhoods or who had experienced severe events that impacted the course of their lives.

The simplified theory of EMDR is that our negative traumatic memories remain in a so-called "dissociated state" in our brain. The emotional impact of the event or events remain out of our conscious control, but when something reminds us of the events, we react automatically with the original emotional charge.

With bilateral stimulation (moving something horizontally back and forth, repeatedly, while the client follows the movement with his eyes), the integration of this memory occurs. The dissociation is substituted by integration, where both hemispheres become involved in the memory. This way the event becomes conscious, it becomes reevaluated, and the emotional intensity decreases.

This is an excellent method to work with, but I had friends who went through this treatment and had a very difficult time after the sessions. The EMDR worked, but my friends had to clench their teeth to be able to endure the horrific memories that came up from their unconscious. They came from families that had tortured them. The memories coming out of the "safe" unconscious storage were overwhelming to them.

Then one day a client who had been coming to me for a while talked about her child, who had begun to hallucinate, was hearing voices, and was seeing things. My client took her to a child therapist who used a method called ETT, where the child looked at rainbow colors while talking. The child became better after a few days of treatment. This was so interesting and promising that I had to learn more about ETT.

This was the beginning of my experience with Emotional Transformation Therapy (ETT), a revolutionary new way of therapy. It does not re-traumatize the victim while the unconscious memory comes up. It is an excellent treatment for those who were abused. As I am learning and applying ETT with more and more clients, I am amazed at how fast they begin to talk about the core of their problems and connect the dots between events they went through. It is astonishing how easily their despair changes into calmness and, lots of times, into joy, empowerment, and wholeness. Resolution is even more rapid when someone wants to work on a problem that causes difficulty in the present but that is not connected to a past event.

If a new method is good, clients who get better will tell others about it. This book is written also to let you know about ETT that is very well known in certain states, including Texas and Oregon, but it still isn't well known in others. These places people are not able to choose it because they have never heard about it.

Another reason I wanted to write this book is for my own sake. ETT is a totally new way of dealing with emotional and physical problems. It is based on several scientific paradigms, and I wanted to understand the basics of it. This book discusses how and why ETT works, while following my journey in discovering and practicing this method. It presents how I was able to understand the theoretical background of ETT. I hope I explain ETT well enough so that others will be able to understand it, as well.

What ETT is not

ETT is not color therapy. "Color" or "Chromotherapy" is used to balance body energy. The Spectro-Chrome therapy invented by Darius Dinshah shines different colored lights on certain body parts in order to physically heal them.

What ETT Is

Steven Vazquez, PhD, introduced ETT about twenty years ago. ETT is a way of doing psychotherapy that uses colors, but in a totally different way. Actually, Dr. Vazquez does not even use the word "color." He uses the words "energy" or "frequency." We observe the visible light with a different energy or frequency as a different color. The real "healer" in ETT is the energy or frequency; the color is only a beautiful addition.

ETT does not shine lights on different parts of the body or manipulate other body parts with the light. ETT works through the eyes, through visual stimulation. Through our eyes, it changes feelings, thinking, which means the brain.

The energy of the light helps the overactive brain function to heal. If the person's physical sickness is psychologically based, even somatic problems can be helped.

Based on its success with a very wide range of emotional issues, ETT is changing the future of psychotherapy. It probably will be the therapy of the twenty-first century. It is more comprehensive and more efficient in targeting and healing negative and painful emotional memories than other therapies. ETT gives relief from the negative messages of our life experiences, changing our self-defeating thought processes through building new connections in our brain.

Since introducing ETT, Dr. Vazquez has been relentlessly trying to perfect it while discovering the riches of this method. In 2012, he published two comprehensive works introducing the theoretical bases and technical execution of ETT. His books are *Emotional Transformation Therapy: An Interactive Ecological Psychotherapy* (Vazquez, 2012b) and *Accelerated Ecological Psychotherapy: ETT Applications for Sleep Disorders, Pain, and Addiction* (Vazquez, 2012a).

Dr. Vazquez includes multiple case studies illustrating how the method is used and displaying the efficacy of this technique. After thousands of success stories, there is enough information about ETT that systematic research has begun recently, and publication of results will follow.

Dr. Vazquez's books and research articles are excellent for professionals. I want to address the general public, the clients themselves, with this book. People need to learn that this totally new type of psychotherapy exists.

Who is this book for?

This book is for those who would like more understanding of how ETT works before they go to an ETT therapist. When someone talks about light-energy, or about looking at different colors during therapy, it may sound strange. People need to have a picture what to expect in a session. I would like to make ETT easy to understand.

Those who have tried ETT usually become fans of it, and I hope that they also will gain a better understanding of it with this book.

ETT's place with other treatments

Drugs and medication

This age is one of quick solutions. Many of us want to take pills when we are sleepy, sad, anxious, or when we don't feel balanced or well. When we're worried, we think Xanax is the solution. When we can't sleep, we think Ambien is needed. When we're sleepy or tired, some form of caffeine "saves the day." These so-called legal drugs can be better than the illegal ones, because sometimes they don't lead to full-blown addiction.

With illegal drugs, the instant mood alteration is available, but the cost is often addiction, which causes long-term suffering for both the addict and their family, and which has financial consequences for both the addict and society. These substances can bring on a feeling of being loved, powerful, in control, "normal," popular, energetic, unafraid, etc. These are basic human desires; all of us would like to have these feelings. But to get them through drugs, alcohol, or other addictions can be quite dangerous and debilitating.

Psychotherapies based on talking

Psychotherapy based on talking can help to change our mood and attitude, teach new coping skills, and reframe our self-defeating thoughts, introducing new explanations for the same events. A good therapist can motivate us to live a more fulfilling life and get along with our family. But the therapy can last for several months, which can be financially daunting as well as time-consuming.

Another shortcoming of talk therapy is that it often deals only with the surface of a problem. As indicated by its name, talk therapy is mainly based on the client's talking about their conscious memories. Most times it does not bring up nor heal really deep, often painful memories that can covertly influence our whole life. It does not touch the core of our issues. These events and feelings become forgotten and join our unconscious memories.

If the root of our beliefs does not change, we might repeat the same unhealthy way of living again and again. Although these beliefs and coping skills were helpful once, they may not fit new situations, which need to be handled in new ways.

Psychoanalytic therapy can cause profound changes, bringing up the unconscious. The problem with this method is that it lasts quite a long time, and the client should have sessions several times a week. The majority of people don't have that much time, nor can they bear the financial burden of lengthy treatment, which can last for years.

Psychotherapy using multiple channels of information exchange

How about a therapy method that uses the same senses that we used to gather information during the time that different events influenced us? We have genetically coded reflexes and our temperament is given, but the majority of our behaviors and thoughts are acquired as a consequence of our contact with the world. We learn about the world through our senses, which are exposed to our surroundings and collect information from them.

Life happens, but we give our experiences their meaning. Observation comes first and interpretation follows. We can say that interpretation is a process of meaning given to an event observed by our senses.

The events don't change. Our observations register smell, sight, voice, and kinesthetic sensations, which are facts. In psychotherapy we want to clarify and change our interpretation of the events. We want to label them with different meanings. In talk therapy our ears are involved. During the session we, the clients, change our interpretation of our experience based on the conversation and what we hear from the therapist.

The majority of the observation in our everyday life does not come through our ears but through our eyes. It only seems logical that the therapist can help to change our interpretation through our visual experiences.

In the majority of Eye Movement Desensitization Reprocessing (EMDR) sessions the therapist uses the client's eyes but not what the client sees. The client follows the therapist's finger or, in more sophisticated practices, white light or other tools which move back and forth between right and left. In this therapy the direction of the eyes is important, not what the eyes look at.

Emotional Transformation Therapy (ETT) uses the direction of the eyes, as well as the light the client looks at. The client and the therapist talk, so the client's hearing is also involved in the process. This communication with the therapist influences the client as well. Thus ETT can have an effect on the client through two channels, through the eyes and ears.

Using these two channels, ETT can be a very fast solution for healing emotional and even certain physical problems. This "healing" can be long-lasting, preventing us from repeating the same dysfunctional patterns in our lives. It can be successful for presenting problems and developmental issues while using fewer sessions than other methods.

Why doesn't every therapist already use ETT?

Why don't people run to use ETT? Why don't therapists, who obviously want to help their clients, line up and demand training in this method?

ETT is still a relatively new method. After thousands of great outcomes in therapy, systematic research has just begun. ETT is a kind of energy therapy that can be grouped with the alternative healing methods that are not taught yet in our schools. The profession has been changing fast, though. EMDR was considered useless a few years ago, but it is the official treatment in many places now, such as at VA Hospitals. ETT will be widely used very soon, as well.

After a therapist hears about ETT, the first question is often, "Isn't it too fast?" ETT can help a client in two to three sessions. There are plenty of reports that ETT worked in just one session. In regular psychotherapy, one, two, or three sessions are used for intake only, not to complete therapy.

The financial ramifications of very rapid therapy can also confuse therapists. They are not greedy, but they have to live on something. How will they pay their bills if clients get well so fast and leave?

I think this confusion will only last for a short time. The turnover may be faster, but more clients will want to be treated with ETT. Why would anyone suffer, when in few sessions their life could become happier and healthier?

Insurance companies will love ETT as well. They don't have to pay for someone's therapy sessions month after month. Those who pay cash will be also very pleased with this short, but profoundly influential, psychotherapy.

Try ETT

The key to the popularity of ETT is experiencing it. The best thing is to go to an ETT therapist and try it. I was hooked when my friend first tried it on me. My clients are the same. The disbelief or hesitation usually lasts till they experience the impact of ETT, when they look at the colors and they experience emotional relief.

With this book, I want to help spread the good news in psychotherapy. There is faster help available that can better peoples' lives. Read this book to understand the basics of ETT and try it with an ETT therapist. Your life will never be the same.

Reading this will give you a better understanding how our vision and brain are involved in our psychological makeup. The more we know about our brain, the more easily we can change dysfunctional habits. Emotional suffering can become temporary.

CHAPTER 1

Understanding Your Brain

Every psychological problem is connected to our brain. That is why we begin our discussion with looking into how it works.

The mind is usually considered the sum of cognition, emotion, sensation, and will. The brain is usually considered the organic representation of the mind. Before going further, please note that the words "mind" and "brain" are used in this book interchangeably.

Connections between brain cells

When we are born, we have billions of neurons. We have more than enough cells in our brain, but we are still not able to vote or make intelligent decisions. The cells are there, but the connections between them are not yet developed. We can move, but our movements are not coordinated. We can make sounds, but they are not speech. The independent neurons have to be connected for the brain to function properly. The connections develop through experiences.

As infants, we give lots of signs about what we feel. When we're hungry, we'll tune ourselves up like we'll die from hunger in the next minute. We can be sad or happy, feel warm or cold, or feel uncomfortable because we're wet. We can feel, but awareness and regulation are missing. We slowly learn how to coordinate parts of our body; focus our attention; talk; and use toys, utensils and so on.

Despite teenagers' sometimes all-knowing attitudes, their understanding and their logical thinking are still only developing. Their brains become complete at about age 24. Until that time we could hang a sign on their foreheads, "Under Construction." Until around age 24, the pruning, specialization, and connection of the brain cells happens. Their experiences mold their brain.

This doesn't mean that our mental abilities plateau or that we necessarily lose our ability to think from age 24–on. Even at older ages our brains are changing, because our circumstances change. Our brains have to make the adjustment. The neurons are established, but the branches of the cells, which are the connections between cells, can grow in number. For this reason, it's good for older people to do or experience things that are new for them. It helps to keep their minds fresh, developing new circuits between the brain cells. The brain has huge adaptability. (Cozolino 2002, XV) With new experiences the mind changes and remains flexible.

Unconscious memories

The different parts of the brain are already present at birth, but the connections between them are not. They come through experiences. We don't need more brain cells to be smart—we need more connections between them. The influences of our emotional and relational surroundings shape our brain starting at or even before birth.

At the beginning of life, when infants don't have words and their cognitive abilities haven't developed yet, the impact of their surroundings on them does not reach conscious understanding. During this time the infants' brains develop circuits based on their feelings and sensations. We can say that the most important learning happens without conscious awareness.

Lots of emotional wounds come from this time of life. These hurts can be intentional, but lots of times they come from an adult misunderstanding an infant's needs. The adult unwittingly can hurt the infant emotionally because of the adult's own issues that are not related to the child.

Psychotherapy is supposed to help to overcome our childhood wounds. Talk therapy can be very good, too, but it is very difficult to reach these unconscious memories with it, because they developed before the child became verbal. The child does not have words for his or her experiences yet.

Selective attention

We are not aware of how much information comes from our environment. Our senses are bombarded with what is going on around us. We are unable to observe everything in its entirety. That means we select only part of the facts of our surrounding world. We experience the world partially. Even the smartest, most observant people can soak up only a certain amount of what is happening around them.

This is a very healthy mechanism of our brain. We have to select what we pay attention to; otherwise our brain would be overwhelmed. We would pay attention to lots of unimportant triggers coming from the environment.

The reticular activating system, which can be found at the brain stem, has the function of determining what gets noticed and what is neglected. This part of the brain selects certain things that it considers important. The rest remains shut out, not only from our conscious but also from our unconscious awareness.

Brain functions

The goal of this book is not to describe brain functions. Nevertheless, I think we should go into a little more details about what is happening in our brain. Our five senses receive information from our environment. From the sensory organs such as the eyes, ears, skin, nose, and mouth, sensory perceptions are transferred to the thalamus, which distributes these neural signals to the sensory cortices.

From these widely distributed and specialized sites, the neural connections lead to the working memory centers in the frontal lobes. Here the sensory information is interpreted to form perception, and is labeled with meaning by integration with other information retrieved from pre-existing memories. The sensations become associated with emotional content from the limbic system.

The amygdala is particularly important in fearful experiences. The amygdala receives the electrical impulses from the frontal cortex, which originally was triggered electrically by the different sensations. When something dangerous happens, the prefrontal cortex becomes inhibited. The prefrontal cortex is the place where complex cognition, planning, organizing, and execution happen. The parietal lobe contains the somatosensory cortex, which gives awareness to the sensations.

In a threatening situation, the senses send signals to the amygdala, but leave out the prefrontal cortex and parietal lobe. This means that the amygdala triggers reactions to the threat without conscious evaluation or even conscious awareness of what is happening. It is a very healthy mechanism, because a quick reaction can be lifesaver.

When the signals go through the amygdala, leaving out the cortices, it doesn't mean that memories don't form. The developing memories are partial; they don't involve every aspect of the experience. These memories serve for quick recognition and remembrance (Beaulieu 2003, 986-988), but details are left out.

In most other situations, the brain processes information in a different way. It uses neural connections from almost every part of the brain to the hippocampus. It involves the prefrontal and parietal cortices as well, which means conscious awareness, planning, and execution are involved.

The hippocampus is a great organizer. It synchronizes the different neural networks, which, depending on the experience, can involve varying parts of the brain. These parts of the brain encode certain components of the experience: sensory, cognitive, and emotional. Connecting the different parts of the experience, the hippocampus coordinates short-term recall.

The signals going through the hippocampus are associated with emotional evaluation. Based on this emotional labeling, the person reacts to or neglects the triggers, sending the right signals to the different parts of the body to act, or to not do anything. Consciousness is involved in these actions.

As we mentioned, both types of neural pathways develop memories. The hippocampal-cortical-based memory has more details, more evaluation, and more awareness (Clugnet and LeDoux 1990). In case of traumatic events that go directly to the amygdala, the memory recording can mainly involve the limbic areas, which are connected to our emotions and the sensory cortices responsible for physical sensations. Awareness is left out.

When we go to a therapist who uses cognitive therapy, these memories cannot be touched or healed, because at the consolidation of these memories the cognition was mainly left out. They remained in us as feelings, such as shame or loneliness, or somatic memories, such as headache, backache, or tension somewhere in our body. In psychotherapy we say that the person has "unfinished business." The energy therapist would say that the energy does not flow freely in the body.

Because traditional psychotherapy does not deal with these experiences, the impact of these traumatizing events and the developed avoidance techniques can remain and repeatedly influence a client's life.

Narrative and traumatic memories

It is important to note the difference between narrative and traumatic memories. Every memory has some kind of emotional component. The narrative memory loses emotional intensity with time. When we fall in love, the world can stop, we do not notice it; we seem to float on air. Later on, we can remember the place, our loved one's eyes, his/her clothes, our surroundings, and even the wonderful feeling. But the intensity of this feeling decreases. We remember that it was good, but we come out of the unreasonable idolization. Our feet touch the ground again. We can say that these memories are hippocampal-cortical memories.

The traumatic memory is different. It is mainly emotional and sensory. When something triggers these memories, we can remember our feelings, the sights, the smells, the touch, the pain, and so on. The traumatic memory does not go through changes with time. It is not processed, or consciously reevaluated. It remains unchanged. No matter how much time has gone by, if something reminds us of that situation our whole body reacts with emotion. Our feeling of unease, for example, remains the same as when the event happened. In these cases the amygdala dominates. The sensory recordings remain and don't integrate with cognitive evaluation. The cortical centers that make the experience conscious are left out.

If the network contains conscious awareness, we can talk about it. If it does not, we have only feelings or sensations, and we don't really understand where they came from.

Art therapy can bring up some unconscious memories. With Eye Movement Integration (EMI) or Eye Movement Desensitization Reprocessing (EMDR) the therapist triggers eye movements that can get in contact with the unconscious memories and reprogram the brain networks, while connecting these memories to conscious awareness. ETT is the newest and possibly the best and most goal-oriented therapy as well as the least traumatizing method for bringing up and healing these traumatic memories. It can work on emotions from an event without cognitive awareness of the event.

Our memory is not localized. It is kept in our brain in a network. The neurons that participated in the observation of the event remain as part of the memory. The smell, sight, voice, feeling, understanding, regulation of our heart, breath, and so on are all information about the event. In the brain they are connected to and characteristic of that experience. If the same or similar situation happens repeatedly, the connections in this network become stronger. If the intensity of the event was considerable, the connections solidify strongly.

Neural connectivity

Because our memory of the event is kept in a network, it is enough to observe a little part of the event, and the whole network can be activated. I often tell my clients, "It is enough to show my little finger to know that it belongs to a human." It is enough to smell a loved one's perfume or aftershave for the person to come to mind. It can even influence our feelings and behavior toward the person who wears that scent.

In his groundbreaking book, *Change Your Brain, Change Your Life: The Breakthrough Program for Conquering Anxiety, Depression, Obsessiveness...*, Dr. Daniel Amen explained that the different behavioral, emotional, or cognitive states impact different brain patterns, or neural connectivity(Amen 1999). In a balanced brain, the discrete impacts from our senses are connected. The experience is put into a healthy perspective with other similar events. In a single-photon emission computed tomography (SPECT) image, the balanced brain is calm, with the same color everywhere.

When we have emotional issues, the brain has overactive and underactive areas. The SPECT image does not show a homogenous organ. One part of the event gets too much attention while other parts are neglected. This is the case when something triggers too much feeling or not enough understanding. The integration (cooperation between the parts) does not become complete. The energy does not flow freely between the different locations of the brain. There is too much activity in certain areas and too little or nothing in others.

If something happens to us and we are not able to process, talk about it, or understand it in a constructive way, the executive functions of our brain won't be involved. The different unprocessed emotions can make and keep part of our brain overactive. Dr. Amen identified the brain areas with his SPECT mapping method, showing irregular activity in certain brain areas when is angry, depressed, anxious, fearful, inattentive, impulsive, worried, obsessed, or experiences many other issues, even eating disorders. After treatment, when the symptoms stop, these brain areas change and have balanced activity.

Sometimes I'm asked, "Why bother with these uncomfortable, hidden memories at all? We can live our lives, forget about the past, and just go forward."

This is true: we can live without emotional healing. We are often not even aware that we have had trauma. We only have migraines, ulcers, insomnia, exhaustion, or other issues that are not totally understandable based on physical conditions. We can be very pleasant people who blow up at home regularly like an overheated pressure cooker. We can lash out at people when they didn't really do anything especially bad to us. We can be painstakingly rigid in our life, paying attention to cleanliness or germ-free surroundings too much. We can become addicted to drugs, food, work, pornography, and so on. We can hook up with an abusive partner again and again.

We can live like that. But why wouldn't we live happier, healthier, and feeling freer and more complete? The repeated problems in life usually come from some background woundedness. We will talk more about this in the chapter on Attachment.

Mental models

The brain is a pattern-seeking machine (Leeds 2010, 45). It develops mental models in order to assess a situation more rapidly and to determine what the next moment in time is most likely to offer (Siegel 2012, 52).

Consider people who suffer from Posttraumatic Stress Disorder (PTSD). For soldiers deployed in a war zone, loud noises—bullets, rockets, explosives—often signal danger and a real possibility of being killed. Responding to true danger with a "fight-or-flight" response is healthy. But when someone who suffers from PTSD hears a loud noise, they are stressed or frightened even when they're not in danger. Hearing even a harmless noise can wake up the fight-or-flight response.

Another example of this automatic reaction comes from my own life. I lived in a country with four seasons. During the winter we didn't have much sunshine or fresh fruit. Almost everyone was tired and vitamin deprived. Now I live in Southern California, where the sky is cloudy only few days a year. Even so, when we have a cloudy day, I feel tired. My eyes see the sky and my body reacts as it used to for years.

Our automatic reactions and habits are not written in stone, even in our brain. We can change them. But how? We will discuss this in the chapter on Chapter 5.

Our brain and somatic symptoms

Another interesting characteristic of the brain that can be used in psychotherapy is the connection between physical pain and emotions. Our brain produces enkephalin, which is a natural pain-killer. When we are in pain, our brain can decrease the pain by producing enkephalin.

The same neural circuit that regulates this pain-killing mechanism is connected to emotional regulation. Both pain and emotional biochemistry influence serotonin, norepinephrine, and neuropeptides such as enkephalin production (Vazquez 2012b, 89). This means the two, pain and emotion, can interact and be influenced at the same time. Consequently, influencing the emotional circuits will have an impact on pain sensation.

The reverse is also true: physical pain can change our emotions. If someone is not able to get closure on painful emotions, it can become physical pain. Laughing with beloved grandchildren can be the best painkiller. On the other hand, grief can become a physical symptom. Everyone has heard cases of long marriages where, when one spouse passes away, the other follows shortly.

This is why ETT can influence, and often end, physical pain while the light-energy targets the emotional suffering. I have had several clients with severe migraine headaches. One I especially remember was almost unable to function, drive a car, or go out to buy groceries because of her daily migraines. When I asked her to sit in front of the light-box, she reacted most to far-red frequencies. I was surprised because these energies are connected to survival, to the life instinct.

When she began to talk about her life, it turned out that she was teased all of her childhood. She learned to have two personas. One persona was for the others, like a mask. The other, the real her, was hidden deeply inside. On the outside she didn't show negative emotions. She didn't give even a little sign of resentment if someone hurt her. Her real emotions were deeply hidden. She lived like two persons.

What is this if not a survival skill? But the "stuffed" or stifled humiliation and feeling of being rejected came out as migraines. When we worked on her ability to accept and express herself, the migraines decreased considerably. She sometimes had headaches, but not the torturous, debilitating migraines.

This does not mean that all suffering is emotionally based. Obviously, there are organic reasons as well. But the intensity and the pattern of pain can be influenced by emotions. One of my other clients had a dull and a sharp pain in her back and neck. The dull pain didn't change, but the sharp one decreased or increased depending on the peripheral light stimulation we used with her. We were able to find the right angle for the light to stop her sharp pain. The pain was psychosomatic.

Pain with an organic origin can be decreased if it has an emotional component. In therapy groups for people with chronic pain, one of the first questions is, "What is the gain having pain?" It may sound insensitive to ask this, but often the person develops an identity based on having pain. This is an unhealthy way to satisfy the person's need for love, belonging, managing anxiety, or the like. If we help the person to recognize this need and find a healthier way to resolve it, the pain may decrease. ETT can be a great tool to discover these usually unconscious hindrances. With the corresponding light the production of natural pain-killers in the body can be enhanced as well.

In the brain the emotions and bodily sensations are connected. There has been a debate about which occurs first: the bodily sensation, which is translated into emotion; or the emotion, which is followed by the bodily sensation. No matter which way it goes, the two seem to be connected.

During our experiences the somatic sensations remain in the somatic memory while the emotions remain as emotional memories. When, for example, the somatic memory is activated, the person can have the corresponding emotions. When the emotion is remembered, the somatic symptoms can be triggered as well.

Because the brain connects the emotional and the somatic information from an experience, if the negative emotion is too intense, it can remain as a somatic memory. People often negatively judge others who have psychosomatic problems. Looking at it from a different perspective, this could have developed originally as a survival skill for people who were not able to verbalize their emotional suffering. Parents often pay attention to their children's physical problems while they don't understand or even neglect the children's hurts. Thus parents can unintentionally "teach" their children to somatize their problems.

The body of one of my clients, who was in a psychiatric hospital, was just like a map of her feelings. She was always pleasant and cheerful, but she suffered from several physical complaints that seemed not to have organic origins. I thought sooner or later we could follow, like a thread, which feeling she was not expressing, based on the location of her physical problems. The woman was in her fifties, and her husband and daughter had passed away. She had moved back to her parents' home. They had criticized her all of her life, demanding that she behave "like a lady," be cheerful, be uncomplaining, and never cry. The woman was a hoarder, as well. Her parents had taught her to somatize her emotions to the point that she needed psychiatric help.

CHAPTER 2

The Electric Memory

Information transfer in the brain

In my mental health groups, I often mention that our different types of thoughts and feelings don't "fly around" in our brain. They become electrical impulses and biochemicals. In the case of depression, for example, our negative thinking pushes certain biochemicals out of balance. Vice versa, when these chemicals are out of balance, our thinking is negative.

Every function of our mind—perception, learning, acting, remembering, and ability—originates in the flow of electrical signals through the neural circuits (Kandel *et al.* 2012, 1699). Discrete brain areas with specific functions are interlinked, building neural networks. These networks make our perceptions, movements, speech, thoughts, memory, and other functions possible. This means that all the healthy and disorderly emotions, behaviors, and cognitions get their origin in the healthy or dysfunctional brain functions (Kandel *et al.* 2012, 2367).

Many people use some form of medication—against sleepiness or sleeplessness, depression or anxiety, and so on. When we take medication, we impact neurotransmitter production and transmission in our brain. The nerve cells (neurons) have specialized cell parts, dendrites and axons, which look like branches. Neurotransmitters are involved in the information transfer only in the small cliff where one brain cell branch meets with another cell branch.

The "medical model" believes that neurochemicals getting out of balance are the reason for different mental and emotional problems. For quite a long time, people have been talking about chemical imbalance in the brain in cases of addiction, bipolar disorder, anxiety, or even depression. The theory is that if the imbalance is in the neurochemicals, then other substances such as drugs or medications can fix it.

That is why "popping pills" has become the most frequent "cure" for our emotional problems. These substances really work. This is why drug- or alcohol-addicted people use their substance of choice to influence the neurotransmitters in their brain. They push the chemicals out of balance to produce pleasure, keep them awake, decrease their anxiety, or feel in control of their lives. The medical model is right, but the substances we take are not specific enough, causing lots of side effects.

Biochemical production is determined by the electrical impulses of the nerve cells (neurons). That means the negative thoughts are somehow connected to these impulses, which influence the biochemicals. The different thoughts, emotions, and sensations travel through the nerve cells via electrical impulses. When a nerve impulse reaches the end of a neuron, a neurotransmitter chemical is released that excites the next neuron. That is why taking different drugs or medications to affect these biochemicals can be good, but maybe there is a better way to influence our emotional problems, by changing the electrical messages in our brain.

The main character of our brain is that it is a continuous energy flow. In fact, every cell in the human body produces and communicates through electrical impulses. Cynthia Graber writes, "we are walking electrical networks" (Graber 2012, 43).

Neurons "communicate" messages through biochemicals at the connection of the cell branches, across the synapses. It is a relatively slow process. The electrical impulses that travel along the nerve branches are much faster. They can reach up till 200 miles per hour (Fields 2009, 19).

If we don't want to solve our problems with medication but to influence the electrical impulses, we have to use some energy. Electrical impulses are the way the brain transfers information. The electrical impulses cause new synapses to develop. Our memory is not localized but exists in these connections.

To change, for example, the emotional content of a memory, we have to change the synaptic connections. This means new connections have to develop or the old ones have to disappear. The change needs energy, which can come from our surroundings. Talk therapy can help to change thinking and restructure neural connections but it is slow and in certain cases ineffective. The most natural energy resource is natural light or its components, which appear as the colors of the rainbow. The different colors have different energy. This energy source has much faster impact.

Genetic predestination

There is an ongoing debate whether nature or nurture determines the character of our life. "Nature" is our genetic makeup. "Nurture" is the influence of the environment on us. If our genes determine our fate, life is "over" for some of us even before it begins. We wouldn't be able to avoid cancer or other illnesses. The most we could do would be to go to a doctor and medicate ourselves to postpone an early end.

On the other hand, if the environment has the most influence on our life, we have some hope that we can change to live a happier, healthier life.

There is a kickback, though. If we are not predestined to a certain type of life but have a choice, we are responsible for the change. We have to take the right steps to change, but it is often not very simple or easy.

Nevertheless, this view of the nurturing environment can give us more choice, and hope in our life and our future. Instead of being almost like a helpless puppet of our genes, we become a "co-creator" of our destiny (Lipton 2005, 226). Thus, even if the genetic predisposition is there, there may be ways to avoid or correct an "unhealthy" genetic inheritance.

Epigenetics is the science of how the signals of the environment regulate gene activity. The "nurturing" influences us through two mechanisms. We have lots of genes but only some of them are activated. Our genetic code does not have to be changed. Through the environment, we can influence which gene is activated and which is not.

Another very encouraging consequence of the "nurture view" is that, if the activity of our cells depends on the impact of the environment, even if the previous influence was damaging, we could change our environment and override the impact—sometimes fully; sometimes at least to a certain extent.

The environment and neurons

Our brain is known as an electrical organ. The environment sends physical signals through our senses to our neurons. These signals are vibrational information such as light, sound, and radio frequencies. The stimulus can be an emotional sensation in the limbic system. The environmental influence impacts the membrane of the cells first. The receptors in the cell walls are protein complexes, which connect the signals of the environment to the answer of the cell.

There are so-called receptor "antennae" vibrating on the surface on the cells such as nerve cells (Lipton 2005, 769). The environmental vibration interacts with the antennae. The simplest picture of this process is that the receptors "read" the energy coming from the environment. The receptors in the cell wall interact with certain molecules, hormones, and other proteins inside of the cell.

The electromagnetic vibrations can regulate DNA, RNA, and protein synthesis. The shape of the different proteins is key to their functions. The electrical energy of the surroundings can change protein shape, which means change in the function of the protein, possibly impacting nerve growth and function.

The photoelectric frequencies (the different colors) fall into the same range as the atoms vibrate in the cell molecules. When they interact they can enhance or cancel each other (Lipton 2005, 1120). Electromagnetic waves, such as the components of natural light, can help to grow new nerve cell connections or help to disconnect them. The changing connections provide the possibility for our brain to work in a more balanced way.

This mechanism is the reason why ETT can be so helpful. ETT uses the colors of the rainbow, representing different electromagnetic energies. The colors can interact with the "antennae" of the neuron walls and influence the cell's biological functions.

Light is not the only thing that influences us. We experience our environment through all five senses. Each of them has an impact on our nervous system. The mechanism is the same: receptors on the neurons receive these messages and change the protein production in the cells themselves. The changed proteins alter the synaptic connections between different neurons. The environmental influence can determine whether certain nerve cells or brain areas are involved, and whether they are integrated into the network that is connected to a given experience or not.

The neural network

Through cell connections, a spider-web-like network develops. This network will be activated repeatedly if the environment provides the same triggers. The more the same event happens, the stronger the connections between cells. This spider web connects nerve cells that were influenced by different part of the experience: sight, smell, touch, etc. Motor neurons and cells providing the emotional appraisal of the event are also part of this network. We cannot tell which cell keeps our memory of an event. Rather, the memory is stored in these cell connections.

Our memory integrates the different senses, feelings, and even the physical reactions that belong to the same event. Because the memory is in the connections, it is enough to trigger one part of the neurons—the others connected to them will be activated as well. That means it is enough to see or sense one part of an event for our mind to recall the whole event. Smelling the perfume or aftershave of a loved ones is often enough for us to think of them.

Often certain painful situations come into the mind as well. If a dog bit us during childhood and it was painful, seeing even a photo of a dog can overwhelm us with fear as an adult. So what happens when someone has PTSD is understandable. Any part of the traumatizing event is enough to trigger the terror of the original event. This can happen years later, in a totally different and peaceful environment. The reaction to even a familiar noise might be consuming fear.

It is fortunate that our brain is flexible and our memory can be modified. Giving new meanings to our experiences can change the connections between our neurons. Old connections can disconnect and new connections can develop. This is the basis for psychological healing.

The "electromagnetic frequencies are a hundred times more efficient in relaying environmental information than physical signals such as hormones, neurotransmitters, (and) growth factors" (Lipton 2005, 1071). Research by Mitch Leslie showed that electrical signals get translated into morphological, or structural, ones. The research used light to trigger synaptic growth of nerve cells on a silicon chip (Leslie 2002, 11). This experiment shows how influential light can be. The different components of the visible light used in ETT are waves with different frequencies or energies. Because cells such as neurons need energy to grow or connect, the light frequencies can influence the nerve cells faster than physical substances such as medications. This is the basis for ETT to have rapid psychological advances, even with the most debilitating problems.

Integration within the brain

Integration, which means connection and free flow of energy, happens between the different parts of the brain horizontally (between right and left hemispheres), vertically (cognitive, emotional, and somatic), and in time (past, present, and expected future).

Sometimes parts of an experience and corresponding parts of the brain that normally would be involved are disconnected. This partial integration happens more often than we think. Our memory can leave out partial or even whole experiences.

Consider, for example, someone who drinks to excess and "blacks out" with temporary amnesia. His cortices, and conscious knowledge, are disconnected. It does not mean he can't walk, talk, or even drive home. But he doesn't have the memory of how he got home. His conscious awareness is left out.

How about husbands who tune out their wives' voices when a favorite football team is playing on TV? They are practicing selective hearing, disconnecting parts of their actual experience.

We also hear about ballet dancers whose legs are severely hurt but who can perform, just to collapse with pain coming off the stage. Here their pain sensation is disconnected from their awareness.

A woman who was attacked while jogging in New York City's Central Park was left unconscious until someone found her covered with leaves. She healed physically, but she is terrified to go back to her regular jogging place, even though she doesn't have any conscious recollection of the event. She says her attacker or attackers could stand beside her and she would not be able to recognize them.

One of my clients was sexually and physically abused from the age of four. I thought I would hear horror stories. It turned out that the client became a thinker who was interested in studying and in achievement at the workplace. She was "flat" emotionally. She "lived in her head." Her emotions became more or less left out from her experiences. If these "missing" parts could be reintegrated, she could change and become emotionally vibrant again.

The difference between earlier and later experiences

According to Freud, our personality is determined by the first five years of our life. Attachment theories agree that the most influential years of our life are the earliest ones. Why do the earlier environmental signals become more influential than the later ones?

One way to understand this is based on our brain's electromagnetic wave profile. We can measure it with EEG. Going down to alpha state means we are relaxed. In hypnosis our brain frequencies slow down to theta or delta waves. They are the lowest frequencies of our brain.

The characteristic brain wave profile changes with age. During their first two years, babies have brain waves mainly in the delta range. When they get older, their dominant brain waves fall in the theta range, until about age six.

When Freud talked about the influential first five years, he didn't know that brain wave studies would later prove that this time is the most suggestible brain-developmental stage of our life. In hypnosis the therapist can suggest things to us while our brain is in theta. In childhood our parents, and to a lesser extent others, can influence or "suggest" how we think about ourselves and the world while our brain is normally in theta. We will discuss this in the Attachment chapter in more details.

The information we observe as a child is downloaded into our mind—with a little stretch, we can say "hypnotized"—and it becomes the major part of our core beliefs, habitual actions, and feelings. The nerve cells build connections based on what we observe, and these paths become "hardwired." These are information-processing paths connecting different parts of the outer world's signals.

Our feelings, thinking, and even our body's physiology are determined by these early "suggestions." Measuring a newborn's brain with magnetoencephalography shows that there are active neural signals building neural paths even at the age of a few days.

Memory is not only the collection of past events. Our memory influences our present and future. Our brain circuits give appraisals of present events and guide our perceptions and expectations.

With age we become less and less suggestible. From ages six through twelve, the alpha waves become dominant in our brain. Alpha waves are the calm, conscious state of the mind. From around twelve years of age, our beta waves slowly become dominant. Beta is the brain frequency when we focus our consciousness on something.

When we remember, we activate these memory spider webs through neural firing. Cells that fire together wire together. This firing can be changed through psychotherapy, causing different wiring. The events in our pasts don't change, but we can give new explanations to them. We can bring different parts of past events into focus. We can change our emotional appraisal of them.

Research has found that, in the brains of children who have lots of positive experiences, the behavioral control, language, memory, and motor skill areas develop an abundance of synaptic connections (Shlain 2012, 413). The same research also mentions that severe, prolonged stress reduces the neural connections in the brain areas that are important in learning and reasoning, while the number of connections increase in the brain areas that are responsible for fear and aggression.

Our experiences impact our brains. In the next chapter we discuss shortly how this happens.

CHAPTER 3

Mirror Neurons

We love it when someone imitates famous people. Though we may not all be able to move, talk, or behave just like rock stars, politicians or actors we all have these abilities to a certain extent.

We mirror others all the time, but we don't notice it. We have been doing this almost from the beginning of our life. This is a basic and very important ability for all of us. This is the way we learn to write or practice different trades. We watch others do something and try to copy them. This is the way of understanding each other, as well.

Our brain has "mirror neurons" that help us to imitate and learn. With their help we can also sense others' emotional states and even their unspoken thoughts.

One of my friends has been married for about thirty years. When they are at a party together, her husband does not have to tell her that he is bored, uncomfortable, or tired. She senses it, and she knows when it's time to leave. They "read" each other's feelings and thoughts.

This doesn't happen just with people who have known each other for a long time. We can walk into a place where people are upset or grieving, and we'll know from the atmosphere that it's time to subdue our joy. Even if we entered in an entirely upbeat mood, we'll soon adjust our behavior to the others in the room. They usually don't have to tell us to change our demeanor.

I was raised in Europe, reading and watching Greek dramas. We learned that they remain meaningful today, because they talk about basic emotions and life situations that are timeless. We don't have to go through the same experiences to understand and empathize. It is enough if we have gone through similar experiences or if we can imagine them. In all of these cases mirror neurons have an important role.

How can we know others? Understanding another person can happen in two ways: through conscious thoughts and through intuition. The first is simple: the other person tells what he or she wants or thinks. It happens through words, through verbal communication.

The message delivered through words can be clear but it is only a small part of our understanding of the other person. Most of the information comes through our intuition. How does it work? This is a nonverbal communication relying on our other senses.

Mirroring and others

We have a mirroring system, which helps us understand others (Keysers 2011, 27). This system is built up from mirror neurons for observing actions and from the part of the brain called the insula lobe, which is responsible for sharing emotions.

The mirror neurons generate the mirror image of the other person's actions in us. We see or hear the other person, and with the help of our mirror system we "translate" the other's behavior and feelings. With the help of the mirror neurons, the brain generates a mirror image of the other person's behavior, facial expression, gestures, movement, and sound in us. In our body the same muscles begin to be impacted, so we can understand the other person's actions. Watching a soccer game we feel how it is to kick the ball.

The insula triggers bodily reactions in us, based on the feelings we observe in the other person. We feel the other person's emotions through having the same bodily feeling that he or she has. This mechanism helps us to have empathy, and feel the other person's feeling.

When we see a smiling face, the muscles in our own face want to pull into a smile, and we think and feel that the other person is happy. Likewise, a sad expression can cause our face and posture to change, while we experience gloomy feelings.

The mirror neurons help to share the other person's actions while the insula participates in shared emotions.

The mirror system helps us to socialize. We are connected to each other with the help of our mirror-system. Our brain resonates with the other person's brain (Keysers 2011, 62).

In other words, we expect others' actions and emotions based on what we would do or feel. By observing others' movements and facial expressions, we predict their goals and intentions based on how we would feel if we had the same bodily movements and facial expressions. We project ourselves onto them. We are no longer independent, but the sight of the other person's movements is mapped in our brain.

A good example of this projection is how children believe that animals behave like them. Animals in children's tales feel and act like the child would feel or act in the same situation. The toy bear has fear and happiness, or is even hungry.

This mechanism of our brain can make our life easier and often safer, for example, when someone senses an attack. When I worked in a psychiatric hospital, a client in the locked unit came toward me in a hall where nobody else was present. I felt a strange feeling, went into a nearby office, and locked the door. This was totally out of my character. A few minutes later, the client attacked a staff member. I didn't know this patient or anything about him. But I sensed, based how he came toward me, that it was not safe to remain in his way.

It can be also quite misleading when we think we know what the other person feels or thinks for sure. The other person can be very different from us. Our mirror neurons often misinterpret others. That's why we have to learn good communication skills.

In marriages, for example, spouses often think they know what the other is thinking or feeling, but they regularly misinterpret them. Little, easily manageable problems can grow into huge fights and deep hurts. Spouses or family members often are not aware that their perception of the other is based on their own feelings. With a little communication, and checking what we observe, lots of misunderstandings and heartbreak could be avoided, and real empathy could develop.

This happens, obviously, between friends as well. I wanted to help one of my friends who has been criticized by her father all of her life. It is not right to have a double relationship, being a friend and someone's therapist at the same time. But I just wanted to help her by having her sit in front of the light-box one time in hopes it would decrease her self-criticism.

It turned out quite differently. She had gone to an energy therapist that week, and while she sat down she was praising the other therapist. She said that this therapist had changed her life and she would like to work with her, sending her clients. She was happy and talkative. I wasn't. I ruminated over this the next few days.

I left this friend a voicemail telling her how much she had hurt me. She didn't understand what my problem was. Because I was too hurt to talk to her in person, she became more and more apologetic, leaving me voicemails and emails asking me for my forgiveness and for some clarification what she had done against me.

I got over my hurt and I was dumbfounded by her heartfelt apology. Originally I thought she knew what I was talking about, but she didn't know that she had hurt me. Her intention was to tell me how much she enjoyed what the other person did. She didn't intend to question the value of what I do.

What happened here? I felt offended with something my friend was not aware of. How does this misunderstanding happen?

When we predict another person's reaction, our brain's emotional and cognitive system gets in connection with our auditory and visual system. It is influenced by what we hear and see. We predict the other's behavior based on what we would do. During this our brain's visual, auditory, and other areas interact and react automatically.

We don't think over logically what the other person does or will do. Our evaluation and prediction of his or her behavior is involuntary at first. We can slow down and think it over and change our prediction, but our first anticipation is automatic. Our consciousness can prevent us from acting while we evaluate the signals coming from the other person.

As we have seen, we misunderstand situations. This is because we have selective attention. There is too much information coming from the world. Our brains select certain stimuli to pay attention to. Our mirror system is at work, but our partial attention determines what it mirrors. In the chapter dealing with attachment issues, we will discuss in detail how our attention develops and often hurts our lives later on. Our partial attention causes us to be self-centered and to often misinterpret others.

How do intuition and conscious thoughts work together? The first thoughts are usually intuitions. With verbal communication, we can refine intuitions and become like members of a good football team. Football players practice different plays many times before a game. They don't have to think any more. They sense where the other player will throw the ball.

Practice makes perfect with mirroring as well. The Hebb rule says that the frequency of the same experience determines how strong the brain connection will be. Neurons that fire together, wire together. This is true both when our intuition is in line with the real message or when we listen to our faulty intuitions. Instead of letting our intuition take over, it would be better to consciously evaluate first.

Mirroring and self-development

The mirror system determines not only how we understand people and the world around us, but has a basic role in child development and in the formation of our self-esteem.

A parent not only takes care of a child's physical needs, he or she shows the child his or her feelings about the child. That becomes the child's identity. An ad on TV showed a teenager with acne who saw mirrors in place of her coworkers' heads. She saw herself in those mirrors all the time.

This is the way we see ourselves through another person's eyes. Who we are depends on who we are in relationship with, and how the important people in our life see us. What is their opinion about us? We see ourselves through their eyes.

We will discuss this in the next chapter, on Attachment, which may provide some explanation of why we developed into the person we are. It may also reveal why we have so many problems.

CHAPTER 4

Attachment

We are social beings. We live with and among people. We couldn't survive alone on an island. It is not by chance that the harshest punishment in prison is solitary confinement.

We don't think about it, but our whole identity develops through our interactions with others over our lifetime. Who we are depends on the other people we have been in relationship with. It's difficult for us to comprehend, but even our personality depends for the most part on other people. Many people are convinced that they don't need other people. They don't understand that even choosing to be cut themselves off from others is the result of previous experiences.

Recently we have heard more and more about attachment issues. Attachment is our relationship with other people. Our basic attachment develops right after we are born with our caregivers, most often our parents.

Our attachment style is based on understanding, or "sensing," the other person's mind. It is called mentalization. The understanding is based not so much on verbal communication as on detection of nonverbal cues.

As an infant, we don't know who we are. Our independent identity hasn't developed yet. While we observe our mother's attitude toward us, we begin to get the picture. We accept her attitude as a true mirror of our self.

Our picture about our self is the one our mother shows us. Our mother's face, tone of voice, gestures, kindness, or rudeness becomes our identity. We internalize how our mother sees us. We look in our mother's eyes like a mirror and believe what we see there. If our mother conveys that we are lovable, we believe it. If our mother neglects or abuses us, we interpret this behavior to believe that we are not worthy of better treatment.

Imagine that we are in a very new place, we don't know the language, our vision is blurry, the noises are confusing, and we don't know what is going on. We haven't developed habits that help us sort out what is important and what is not. It can be very anxiety provoking.

We come into the world like that, as infants. We can become overstimulated very easily. Not only can the bad experiences be too much, but the good ones can be too much, as well. We may enjoy a little tickling, but too much tickling causes uncomfortable grimacing. We may love to gaze in our mother's eyes, but after a short time we may need to turn away.

One of the main jobs of a mother is to decrease her baby's and then her child's anxiety or overstimulation. If a mother does not provide understanding, validation, and calm surroundings, her child will have to develop self-defense methods to decrease his anxiety.

Based on a mother's reaction, the child's personality, feelings, and coping skills develop. Babies, children, and usually even adults go the direction where they can feel good or at least avoid negative feelings. Relationship styles and the child's personality develop during these interactions. If the mother provides a calming reflection to her child's experiences, the child becomes calmer, feels safer, and will look for further closeness to the mother.

Not to be understood causes narcissistic wounds. A child's self-esteem decreases because of these wounds. Parents usually don't want to cause negativity in a child, but they do anyway. The child is not developed enough to reason out why his parents behave as they do.

If a mother does not understand her child's inner experiences, such as fear, hunger, or anxiety, it can confuse the child. The child tries to be understood. Research has shown that one way to get the right answer from a mother who under-reflects the child's signals is for the child to enhance their behavior to elicit a reaction from her (Fonagy *et al.* 2003, 685). The child wants to have some validation, some harmony between his inner, physiological sensations and his mother's projected feelings. The child begins to overreact, just like a child who has a temper tantrum. If his mother does not react, the child's first reaction is to scream louder.

There are other unhealthy reactions when a mother overreacts to her child's feelings. The child's anxiety won't be calmed, but enhanced. Fear can also be evoked if the mother reflects too precisely to the child's signals. A child learns how to relate to self and to others during these interactions.

A child's attachment style develops during interactions with his or her parents and caregivers.

Here are a few main attachment styles. The healthiest one is the secure style. This is an ideal relationship, but not too many people have it. The main characteristic of the person who has a secure attachment profile is that he or she can be called a "being."

How does the secure attachment style develop? How do we become (human) "beings?"

When a baby is born, a mother surrounds her newborn with love. But love is not enough. The mother has to understand her baby's signals. When the mother "gets" what is happening with and in her baby, she reacts accordingly. When her baby is hungry, she feeds him. When her baby is anxious, she comforts him. The healthy attunement means that the mother can read her baby and acts with love and care, with right understanding, and in a timely manner, so that she decreases her baby's anxiety.

Mary Aintsworth recorded interactions between babies and their mothers. When she slowed down the recordings, there was a real, nonverbal communication between the babies and mothers.

When a mother understands her baby and reacts accordingly, the baby begins to feel more and more comfortable and secure. He feels loved and cared for. He begins to develop good self-esteem. This is not because he is necessarily an extraordinary talent or handsome. The self-esteem comes from the mother's' behavior, from her right attunement to him. The mother's understanding and reaction makes the baby feel not only understood but important as well. The baby becomes "securely attached" to his mother.

When the securely attached child has grown a little older, his mother disciplines him. The child needs it because he does not inherently know what is right and wrong, what is good or dangerous. Loving the child does not mean letting him do whatever he wants to do. The child has to learn new skills, boundaries, and moral values. His mental abilities are not developed enough to make his own decisions independently. His mother has to guide, give limits to, and correct his actions.

In the meantime, the mother of a securely attached child assures him that he is loved unconditionally—no matter what. The mother corrects her child's behavior, but she does not criticize his personality. Because the securely attached child does not experience rejection from his mother, he will be able to ask when he is in need, confess when he made a mistake, and show when he is happy. The child remains open to and communicates his inner thoughts and feelings with his mother and later with others. He accepts help and correction.

A mother of a securely attached child pays attention to her child. She tries to discover his talents and abilities. She tries to bring out what is best in the child. Thanks to his mother, his self-esteem continually grows.

A securely attached child will have good friends, because he is not needy for love. He has that love from his mother. He does not become a bully, because he does not have to feel powerful through belittling others. He knows that he is loved, cared for, and cherished.

The securely attached child's positive experiences usually continue in school and with teachers. He can concentrate in class. He can be kind and affectionate and comfortable with himself. He will have good partners and friends.

A securely attached teenager does not beg for love. He can manage if someone does not want to go out with him. He knows that there are others who will. He doesn't want to date someone who can't live without him. He doesn't tend to get enmeshed with emotionally wounded partners.

A securely attached adult is aware of his needs and able to work patiently to satisfy them. The self-imposed delay of gratification is the main characteristic of healthy emotional self-regulation. Those who can delay gratification have hope and endurance.

A securely attached adult has hope in life. He can have fun, knows what he wants, remains flexible and assertive, and maintains his boundaries. He accepts himself as he is. He can live in the present, and does not pull the baggage of the past. He has internal value and he knows it.

(In order to simplify the explanation I left out the the other parent's role. His/her impact is also very important in the child development.)

Very few of us are like this. We can call these people "beings."

Not Ideal Attachment: (human) "Doers"

The majority of us are "doers." We feel good about ourselves when we are able to do something: we have a good job, education, athletic skills, cooking abilities, and so on. These things are important, but these are external values. We think of ourselves as important for what we do or have instead of for who we are.

One of my most painful memories is of a young client who had schizophrenia and was looking for a job. Nobody wanted to employ him. He finally told an interviewer that the company would get a tax refund if he worked there. It was heartbreaking to hear. This is the epitome of someone who does not feel valuable as a person. The other party gains something because of a something extraneous to him, which becomes his value. What if he loses his job, or gets sick? Would he become worthless? It is very sad, but there are lots of us who sometimes feel the same way.

We should feel good about ourselves because we were born, just because we "are." To have good feelings about ourselves is our birthright. Externalized value generally comes from an upbringing that is not ideal and from interactions with emotionally unhealthy people.

I don't want to criticize parents. They usually do the best they can. Their lives are not that simple. They have to work long hours, pay the bills, and endure sickness, unemployment, difficult bosses, unfaithful spouses, and so on—not to mention the fact that they were possibly raised themselves in a way that was not ideal. How could they give what they have never received?

Parents often adjust to their culture. They may push their children to behave or become someone based on what the culture values. They want to make their children's lives easier, but they can unknowingly reject who their children really are.

The father of one of my clients has an electrical repair business that my client is supposed to inherit. But my client loves art and hates electrical repair. He is an artist who has not dared to stand up for himself against the family's demands. He hates his life and feels like a failure. He wants to measure up to something he is not.

Those who don't have the hope to become who they really are and those who are ashamed of themselves often don't have healthy emotional self-regulation. They may turn to drugs or alcohol or other addictions. These people don't hope to be appreciated as "beings." The delay of gratification does not work, because they don't think eventual gratification is possible. Addiction can give some kind of high right away, some kind of good feelings about themselves. Their value is outside of them.

How Does the "Not Ideal Attachment" Develop?

Like secure attachment, "not ideal" attachment is the result of a process. In the case of "not ideal attachment," a baby signals some need: hungry, tired, sleepy, and so on. The mother does not understand the child, gets angry, or does not pay attention. Put another way, the mother is not attuned to the child. For example, the baby might like to play and have eye contact, producing good feelings, but the mother may be on the phone and not paying attention.

I have worked with women who had drug addictions. They told me that their children were often locked out of the room while they were trying to get high. The children could cry or beg, but they brushed their children off. They focused on getting high.

A mother might laugh about or tease the child for his behavior, which can be uncomfortable for the child. The mother doesn't necessarily do this to hurt her child. She may simply be in her own world and not understand her child's needs. Adults often think, the child does not understand the insensitive jokes, or when the adult reveals something about the child which is intimate to him.

If mis-attunement happens only a few times, no real problem occurs. But a mother has a habitual way of living with and relating to her child. When a child is regularly misunderstood or mistreated, and when a mother's reactions regularly are not in line with her child's sensations, anxiety develops.

To protect himself and to decrease his anxiety, a child may lower his own value in his own mind. The dissonance decreases between the mother's response and the child's expectations if he believes he deserves the mother's reaction. A child is self-centered. He begins to feel that the problem is with him. He begins to feel shame.

This is a very healthy self-protection at a young age. A child idealizes his mother. It gives him security to belong to someone who is powerful and good. It would be extremely anxiety- and fear-provoking to believe that his mother is antisocial or something similarly negative when his life depends on her. By lowering his own self-worth, the child does not have to change his idealization of his mother. The shame decreases anxiety.

Shame is thought to be based on the activation of the parasympathetic system, which helps the body calm down (Siegel 2012, 312). Shame decreases anxiety, but a child can become stuck in his negative self-perception. A child's brain looks for patterns. This self-perception becomes part of a pattern that can damage the child for the rest of his life.

The other way to decrease anxiety is for a child to adjust to his mother. He begins to pay attention to the mother, to when and how to signal that he has some needs. He tries to leave the mother out of his problems as often as possible. He tries to forget about his own needs, or learns to satisfy his needs himself. He learns not only that he is not the "center of the universe," but that he is the one who must adjust to his mother if he does not want to feel rejected or neglected again and again.

What we live is what we know. We think the way our family lives is normal. Even if we later find out that our family life was messed up, our thinking, beliefs, and coping skills develop based on how we grew up.

A mother may have preconceived expectations toward her child. She may want her child to adjust to her time, attention, requirements, and emotional state. When a child does what the mother wants, the child is "likable" and not rejected or reprimanded. The child learns to adjust and become a face-reader, mind reader, and doer of the mother's will.

The "doer" child decreases his feeling of being rejected by adjusting to the mother. The child does not understand that the mother is supposed to understand and adjust to her child. The child begins to hide his real needs because the rejection is unbearable. The mother's needs become more important to the child than his own needs.

I remember a client who had huge social anxiety. He became sweaty even when thinking about opening his mouth at a job interview. His father was a raging man. When the child talked at the "wrong time," his father became rude and threatening. The boy was scared to ask even for a sandwich when he was hungry, for fear of his father's angry outbursts.

A child cannot pack his backpack and move to a neighbor's house. He does not even know whether the neighbors are different. Even if they are different, the child feels he "deserves" his mother's treatment. He has to remain in his home with the people who raise him. His life depends on whether he can adjust to his mother's personality and actions.

A child senses how his mother feels about him and believes that this is "him." As we mentioned, in secure attachment, healthy self-esteem develops. Every other attachment style leads to some kind of shame feeling, such as being not acceptable, not being enough, or not being lovable.

This is like the Stockholm syndrome. This phenomena was introduced after terrorists took over a plane filled with passengers and demanded the freedom of their imprisoned group members. To make their point they began to kill passengers. The hijacked passengers' lives depended on the terrorists. They could not escape. They began to side with the terrorists. They became convinced that the terrorists were right.

This is a survival mechanism. If someone cannot fight the enemy, lots of times they become an ally with the enemy and agree with them. If the mother does not show love, the child believes that he is not lovable.

I know that this is a very rough example for the majority of families, but it may illustrate what is going on in the child. The mother does not necessarily want to reject the child, but she may follow her own agenda instead adjusting her agenda to the child's needs and signals.

The child learns to behave as expected in order to get some attention. He becomes a "doer." He is valued when he does the "right" thing. This "pleasing" behavior becomes a habit and will continue in other relationships as well. He can become a pleaser who adjusts to others and gets his self-esteem from how well he can do that. He is not open with his desires or problems. He becomes more and more self-reliant with his needs.

People misunderstand this kind of turning-inward behavior. They think this is independence. This kind of "independence" means: I don't trust anyone. They will hurt me or shame me somehow if I ask for help. I can rely only on myself. Lots of times this self-sufficiency is so ingrained that it does not even occur to the person to ask someone for help or advice. This is woundedness, not independence. The child may become passive-aggressive, pleasing others while manipulating them to do what he wants instead of asking for it. Real independence is when someone knows what he can do, and when he needs help, he is able to ask for it.

The child can learn just the opposite behavior if he does not get attention unless he acts out. To be a "bad boy" can be painful, but it is better than being nonexistent. Because he sees himself in the eyes of others, he begins to believe that he is really "bad" and continues to live up to it, while his self-esteem could not be worse.

There are "invisible children" as well. If the pleasing does not help and the acting out becomes too painful, "disappearing" becomes the way. The child begins to explain to himself that his needs are not important. He is not important. He becomes emotionally numb. The problem is that to be invisible is totally against our human nature. These children often turn to drugs or cut themselves to feel alive.

Similar people attract each other. The "doer" child won't usually end up with a "being" child. They don't have many issues in common. If a child is ashamed of himself, he won't have anything to tell someone who is "OK." If they become friends, the "wounded one" still won't open up. He becomes the seemingly balanced one who is independent enough to solve his otherwise "not very serious problems."

The "doer" child feels comfortable with other "doer" children. They understand each other. These children can be very good at sports or in school, but they still don't feel good about themselves. Their value is not in themselves, but in what they are doing.

Later the partner choice suffers as well. Intimacy comes from shared weaknesses. If one partner dares to open up and the other partner still loves them, they can become intimate. But how can someone love the real person of a "doer"? He dares to talk about himself only to someone who also came from "unhealthy" circumstances. When two people come from an unhealthy world, how do they know how to build a healthy relationship? Where do they learn it? It can be very difficult. Both of them would like to heal, but usually instead of supporting and understanding each other they may misunderstand and hurt the other.

CHAPTER 5

More Characteristics of Unhealthy Attachment Styles

Between birth and five years a child's ruling brain waves are theta and delta. In hypnosis people go down to these brain wave stages, where people are the most suggestible. That means the child learns the mother's "messages" as valid. The mother's reaction gives meaning to the child's sensations. If the mother neglects or gets angry when the child is afraid, the child learns to disconnect from these signals of his body. The child learns not to accept certain physical sensations. Anger becomes nonexistent, for example, in lots of girls. A child can learn a different explanation for their emotion based on the mother's reaction. Fear can become a sign of weakness for lots of little boys.

The child begins to behave. They learn not to cry or laugh or whatever the mother does not validate. I had a client who was beaten as a baby when she dared to cry. She is 55 years old now and still becomes numb when the circumstances would make anyone else cry.

We gain information about a person's attachment style when we observe how he deals with his emotions (Siegel 2012, 10). In the case of secure attachment, the person is aware of his feelings and dares to express them.

When the childrearing was not ideal, the child develops coping mechanisms and emotional regulation to avoid or decrease the hurt. The person having other types of attachment has limitations in recognizing, accepting, and expressing certain feelings. These characteristics usually develop in childhood, but lots of times remain in adulthood as well.

I want to introduce few attachment styles. The following list is not complete: there are more. I just want to illustrate how our attachment styles determine our everyday lives, causing psychological problems for us and for the people around us.

Nonsecure attachments

Avoidant/dismissive emotional regulation

People with this kind of attachment style try to limit their feelings. This is true mainly for unpleasant emotions, but they feel less happiness and other pleasant feelings as well. People who deal with their anxiety this way can be very successful as professionals, but they still don't live their lives to the fullest. It is a limited way of living.

Just ask the woman who is married to this kind of man. He shows no romantic feelings, no understanding of other emotional reactions. This kind of spouse can be a very good provider. Nevertheless, intimacy without emotions can be very difficult. Avoidant people didn't develop skills for how to face feelings. Emotions cause too much anxiety and insecurity.

Feelings are information about our surroundings and messages from life. Avoidant people leave out lots of the guidance that circumstances give them. How can people really connect to someone who is distancing when pleasant or unpleasant emotions occur? They can remain very alone and they leave their family members emotionally deprived.

Lots of workaholics are like this. They are good at work—they know what to do there. But dealing with the feelings of their personal life makes them uncomfortable. They learned early on to shut their emotions out of awareness because there wasn't a way to deal with them otherwise. Nobody validated them or showed them how to react.

When you talk to a person who is avoidant, they seem to have a great life. They often disregard negativity in their family's life. It is true for them because their self-protection leads them to dismiss what contradicts the idealized fantasy of their life. They often don't remember their childhood, so they don't have to be aware of negative experiences.

Fearful/avoidant

The person with this attachment style has low self-esteem. He didn't learn that he is worthy of being loved. He has feelings. He would love to have intimate relationships but his insecurity makes it very difficult. He does not trust that the partner won't reject, use, or humiliate him. The person lives in contradictions. He can have separation anxiety while he tries to reject the person who can reject him.

People who have this kind of style would like to have close intimate relationships, but they have had bad experiences with them. Lots of abusers have this kind of attachment style. They live in a relationship the way the violence circle shows. Their relationship has a honeymoon stage, when they are the most loving person. After a while tension begins to build up in them, and sooner or later they become verbally and/or physically abusive. The remorse and the honeymoon stage follow. He "cannot live" without a partner, but he has to humiliate her before she would humiliate him.

Resistant/ambivalent or anxious/preoccupied

This is the emotional regulation style of a person who is "too emotional." He is clingy and anxious. There is constant fear of losing the relationship. This person can be jealous without real cause. He is regularly on an emotional roller coaster. He can be too dramatic, even suicidal.

Everyone knows couples who break up almost violently and make out passionately. They cannot live with or without each other. Their family can live in constant crisis. There is not much peace. Everything is overreacted to in both positive and negative ways.

Disinhibited or undifferentiated

This attachment style is characterized with shallow emotional connections, without discrimination. This person can talk about his deepest intimate problems to whoever listens to him. He is like a child who was in several foster care homes at a very early age and tries to connect with and be sweet to everyone. These people can be in danger of falling victim to abusers. They cannot differentiate between safe and unsafe partners.

One of my clients moved to another state because an old boyfriend wrote her a letter. She thought he wanted to marry her. After leaving everything behind, she had to wake up to the fact that the man had a long-term girlfriend and he was only interested in some concrete question. My client fell in love with someone else without delay.

Preoccupied attachment style

Role reversal/codependency

One type of preoccupied attachment style can be seen when there is role reversal. These people were "parentified" as children. They took care of the emotional needs of their parents and they continue this behavior as adults. They are the ones who take care of everyone else while neglecting themselves. They are the real codependents. They are too responsible for others. They solve others' problems and feel others' feelings. They don't know themselves. They don't know what they like or how to care for themselves. Their value is in how much they can serve others. They feel the other's feelings too much, often more than the other person himself.

I heard a joke about codependent people: It's said that you see your whole life flashing before your eyes when you think you're about to die—but a codependent sees the other person's life flashing before their eyes. The codependent's identity is determined by how much she/he can adjust, understand, solve, and take over responsibility and pain from the other. ALANON groups are full of codependent people. They are wrong because they don't understand who the addict is and what their responsibility is. They become enablers.

Exaggerated attachment style

The other preoccupied attachment style is the exaggerated one. This type falls head over heels in relationships in an instant. They are loyal and idealize the other person. They can become people pleasers just to keep the other person close to them. They find their value in being connected to someone they think is better than them.

Special Avoidant Attachment Style

Psychosomatic

With psychosomatic avoidant behavior, the emotions are not faced or even felt, but the person's emotional signals turn into physical ones. We often downgrade people who have psychosomatic problems. But they can be the result of not being heard otherwise. When a child does not get attention unless he has some physical sickness, he can learn to "feel" with his body. Eating disorders, migraines, and stomach problems can be the sign of this kind of attachment.

Other subcategories of the different main classes of attachment are found in other resources (Vazquez 2012, 45).

Attachment styles as messages

The attachment styles are the ways that we think about ourselves, other people, and about our abilities to begin and be in relationships. They are "messages" of the past that we repeatedly unconsciously tell ourselves. If it is the secure type, we are lucky. We "tell" ourselves good, empowering self-talks. Other attachment styles give us different negative "messages."

We filter everything through our way of thinking, basically through our attachment style. It develops mental models that guide our attention to certain things and gives meaning to what we experience.

In groups I often mention that if someone has negative self talk and a hundred things happen to him, if ninety nine are good and one is not that good, he will pay attention to the one that is not that good and neglect the other ninety nine. Thus we can become overwhelmed by that event that otherwise would not deserve much attention.

We live in the present, but our past influences how we perceive the present.

These "messages" have a huge impact not only on our present but on our future, as well. How can someone become successful with a negative, discouraging mentality? The majority of problems people bring to therapy sessions have their roots in these messages.

The person who has secure attachment style can react emotionally and cognitively as well as in his behavior to the present issue. He does not carry emotional, unfinished baggage. Those with other attachment styles react to the present issue with a mixture of present and past emotions and thoughts.

Professor Feinberg writes that defense mechanisms developed in childhood repeatedly appear during our life (Feinberg 2009, 51). This becomes more obvious when we are under pressure. More automatic mechanisms kick in. The stress can decrease our cognitive control. In this case our consciousness is often turned down and the automatic regulation of habits, our unconscious, guides us.

We mentioned that we cannot pay attention to everything. Our attention is guided by the "messages" of our mental filter. Because a person pays attention to his "mental model," he gets more and more proof that he sees the event properly. So, misunderstanding the situation, he gets hurt again and again. In the meantime he hurts others repeatedly by his attitude and behavior. The person thinks he reacts to the present situation, but he sees everything through a distorted filter. He perceives the world as a mixture of the present and the past.

Social referencing

The early attachment deeply impacts not only the child's self-esteem but every area of life. He will begin to base his attitude toward other people and life in general on observing what the caregiver/mother does. This is called "social referencing." When the child is not sure how to react to a situation, he looks at the mother for guidance. It can change over time, but there is a brain development basis to the saying, "Look at the mother and marry the daughter." The daughter will be often similar to the mother.

Relationships hurt and they can heal, as well. We think we would like to be happy, but we look for familiar situations. Familiarity brings a sense of safety and security, even if it is a false one. We become habitual in our understanding of others, the type of people we choose, how we react to them, and how we explain situations. We pick people we feel connected to and who are like us, not healthier ones or those who would be able to heal us.

The memories can lead to a self-defeating attitude: the child and later the adult feels that he was not worthy of care or protection, or that he deserved the neglect or mistreatment. These mental models can last into adulthood. The person will expect that others are unloving, critical, and unsafe. Actually he seeks out people like that, not because he wants to, but because these are familiar behaviors. He knows how to react to them. It does not occur to him that he repeatedly does the same things expecting other outcomes.

The person develops coping skills to live his life based on his mental models, seeing ghosts even when there are none. This is the explanation of the self-fulfilling prophecy. These children and later adults have difficulty building a support system that would help them. They are often unable to notice and protect themselves in dangerous or unhealthy circumstances.

How many times have we heard of people who were molested as a child and then raped, often repeatedly, as an adult? Their conscious mind was not involved in the appraisal of the molestation and cannot prepare them to recognize the warning signs later. Nobody helped them to understand that they were victims. If they feel that they deserved the mistreatment, or they were responsible, they won't avoid the unhealthy relationships later. They don't see abusers as they really are.

In secure attachment the parent or caregiver understood the baby's signals and reacted accordingly. The child felt understood and self-esteem and security grew. Securely attached people are open to good relationships, and they recognize when someone is not healthy for them.

Avoidantly attached children may dismiss close relationships in the future. They can become controlling. They learned not to rely on others. Children who were mistreated may have social anxiety in the future. Their connection with the mother was contradictory, so they don't know what to expect. They try to pursue the mother to help them calm down and feel secure. This unpredictable connection strengthened the child's need for the mother. They can pursue partners who are unloving toward them recreating the original scenario in order to heal the wound.

Can we have more than one attachment style?

A child can have different types of attachment to each of his parents. He can be securely attached to his mother and avoid ant with his father. In fact, a person's behavior or feelings change depending on whom he is talking to or meeting at a particular time. The person who is securely attached remains authentic. He may talk differently and show different parts of his personality to his wife or coworkers, but this "style change" is not rigid. He has an authentic self, and he does not change drastically.

The experiences with one person develop certain neural networks and the experiences with another person develop others. These networks are connected, not rigidly separated, so the energy flow is free in time in a person's spider-web-like neuronal connections. We can say that the private and public selves are in harmony. The public self is the adaption to the outside world. The private self is the inner one.

If someone had to adjust to a less healthy upbringing, the networks he developed are self-protective and rigid. His "selves" can be very different. The experiences with different people remain in separated networks, with no free-flowing energy.

For example, the family of an alcoholic has a lot of trouble inside the home, while outside they want to show a perfect family image. The private and public selves have become distant. They have a lot of secrets, and are afraid of criticism and humiliation. They learn not to tell anyone or trust anyone, and operate at a certain anxiety level all the time. The energy flow between the "selves" is not free.

The person's inflexibility can be apparent mainly in his personal life, in his close relationships. The emotional charge is higher with our relatives and "loved ones" than with people we don't have close relationship with, so the person can be a pleasant person in public and very difficult to live with at home. Marriage, for example, can bring up lots of unfinished emotional issues. Adult children of alcoholics for example can be much less emotional in public situations and deeply sensitive to little emotional hurts at home.

Brain development and attachment style

Daniel Siegel says, "The different patterns of child-parent attachment are associated with differing physiological responses, ways of seeing the world and interpersonal relationship patterns." (Siegel 2012, 4). "The emotional responsiveness may be the primary means by which these attachment experiences shape the developing mind. Emotions are the central organizing processes within the brain." We will discuss the role of emotions in detail in the next chapter.

A person's ability to organize emotions directly shapes the ability of the mind to integrate experiences and adapt to future stressors. The ability to integrate emotions is mainly the product of earlier attachment relationships.

In cases of secure attachment the energy can flow freely in the connections and between the two hemispheres as well as the different parts of the hemispheres. There is awareness and understanding. The parent rightly attuning to the baby and mirroring him or her can build healthy neural integration, which results in secure attachment.

On the other hand, the person can become "stuck" when the experience remains mainly in one hemisphere. This can occur when the person tries not to pay attention or explain what is happening with him, or when the experience is too disturbing. In this case the energy between the parts of the brain is not flowing freely. The integration does not happen between the brain areas responsible for registering somatic, emotional, and cognitive parts of the experience. The limitation of the energy flow causes stress.

As we discussed in previous chapters, if the spiderweb connection is already established, the same experiences can activate the same neurons and the synaptic connections can become stronger. The earlier experiences influence gene expression, which determines the connection of the neurons. If the connection is stronger, it will be more and more difficult to avoid the path and build new connections based on new environmental messages.

Although this kind of change in our neural connectivity happens throughout our life, our earliest experiences have the strongest impact on our brain. Our early experiences strengthen these networks so many times that they became automatic, which means unconscious. The unconscious connections are stronger than the conscious ones. That is why early experiences can determine how our brain processes our later experiences.

If a mother was depressed during the first year of her child's life, she cannot react with open joy to her child. Not only will the mother's brain show decreased left frontal brain activity because of her depression, but the infant's brain will show decreased left frontal brain activity, as well. The right frontal activity is increased in both of them (Siegel 2012, 178).

Later in life those who have left hemisphere dominance have problems understanding nonverbal messages, reading faces or gestures, or sensing others' or even their own emotions. Avoidant people can have a domineering left hemisphere while anxious people are more right-hemisphere dominant.

The right hemisphere helps to read others. It gives a more holistic understanding of others.

Habit formation

As we mentioned, memories of repeated events perceived in early age can become unconscious and generalized. Our brain likes to find and follow patterns. It works very economically. Once it discovers a pattern, our brain doesn't have to pay close attention to it any more. It can go to the next event.

These patterns are generalizations, the so-called "mental models" that are the way we think, feel, react to others, or see ourselves. These mental models are necessary to make our lives easier. They help us to predict and react to present and future situations. The problem is when the mental models are based on an unhealthy integration of past events and relationships. In that case the adaptation to the present life is distorted. All of us see our lives, others, and our futures through the filter of our mental models, through the generalizations of our brain.

The mental models serve as anticipation. The secure child will predict that pleasant things will happen to him. People have been pleasant to him, after all. He has hope and trust. The insecurely attached child's expectation for people and for the future is not that good. People and life can be uncontrollable, fearful, or anxiety-provoking at a minimum.

The mental models appear as learned behaviors, as well, helping or hindering our lives. Research on trauma patients shows that the brain's right hemisphere keeps our emotional memories. When such memories are recalled, the right part of the brain shows activity. These traumatic memories are not integrated with the left, more logical, hemisphere. These more emotional memories without logical appraisals will determine the person's feelings and behavior. The generalizations work automatically. A tire blowing up can cause a vivid flashback for somebody with war-related PTSD.

We can say that self-regulation, which is connected to emotional intelligence, depends on the integration of the brain. A healthy upbringing helps self-regulation. An upbringing involving abuse or neglect hinders emotional intelligence.

The self-regulation that develops does not change easily in later years, even when the circumstances are different. The person's relational skills can become dysfunctional, meaning that the person does not adjust appropriately to a given situation.

Lipton writes that a cell cannot grow and protect itself at the same time (Lipton 2005, 1435). It is "either/or." For a human being, this means that either the unconscious or the conscious gets signals from the environment. Our mind either protects us or grows.

For example, we get energy from our food. The developed energy first activates our self-protection, to avoid danger regardless of whether it is real or perceived. Focused attention conveys energy. If I think people use or misuse me, and I cannot trust anyone, I will protect myself. The feelings of being free, happy, healthy, loved, supported, and satisfied with my life are stunted.

Our energy first goes to surviving stress-producing circumstances. If the stress lasts long, the body's immune system weakens and different illnesses can attack us. Our conscious mind could help, but our thinking ability shuts down to give place to the automatic unconscious. We don't develop our abilities when we're trying to survive. We stop being creative or even thinking clearly. Even our muscles become weaker.

The unconscious develops as a reaction to experiences, even from before the time we were born. I had a client who felt unloved almost all the time. She suffered from loneliness, despite several friends who were there for her no matter what. It turned out that her mother had wanted to abort her. There is more and more research about how much an infant hears and feels in the mother's womb. My client's heartbreaking feeling of being unloved may have originated from her experiences in her mother's womb.

We people tend to judge each other for what we do. We can be very harsh and unforgiving. We often forget to check why a person acts the way he does. It may be a learned behavior from those who had an important influence on him. The wrong skills may have been developed to survive unhealthy circumstances, based on the opportunities he had then. If nobody was there to comfort him or help to change the situation, he did what he could do. He didn't know that these behaviors wouldn't be helpful or appreciated in later years under different circumstances. At the time, they helped him achieve his goal to survive.

It is important to understand this because children coming from miserable circumstances often fall short in educational achievement, causing more negativity later in their lives. Many high school dropouts have not had a balanced home life. They may be living in "survival mode." Their brain works to decrease anxiety and does not have the energy to concentrate on learning at school.

If the unconscious is negatively programmed, it can signal danger, shame, or disrespect even if the situation doesn't warrant it. It's difficult to override unconscious messages, because the unconscious becomes like a translation system. If something contradicts the translation, our minds try to dismiss it.

The problem is when these survival skills have become unconscious and habitual. When something triggers bad feelings, the person reacts habitually and automatically, not thinking about whether his reaction to the present situation is appropriate. Other people's judgments can make his life even more miserable. He has not conformed to the new and possibly healthier circumstances, or taken into consideration that he's not a child any more. He could stand up for himself or leave those who are no longer right for him. To change what worked before usually means self-awareness and asking for help.

Healing

We can overcome habitual patterns. Emotional growth can happen if we can become flexible and are able to heal from earlier relational wounds.

A good relationship would be able to help in healing, but we usually end up with another "wounded" person.

Cognitive therapy and positive psychology have their advantages, but they work mainly with conscious events.

The conscious mind is often overridden by the unconscious one. It is much more influential and it is automatic, much faster than the conscious mind. As Lipton writes, the "subconscious mind processes 20,000,000 environmental stimuli per second versus the 40 environmental stimuli interpreted by the conscious mind in the same second ... ." (Lipton 2005, 1656).

This means that positive thinking or changing the cognition is useful, but mainly when the person's subconscious does not contradict the conscious. Due to the memory network, it is enough to perceive a little part of the experience that reminds us of some earlier bad memory to trigger the unconscious reaction. Thinking positively is not enough. We have to change our unconscious to be in line with our conscious.

If we discover the core of our patterns, we can recognize the misperception and not continue the patterns. But it is not that simple. Unless we get healed from the emotional consequences of the events that formed us, we will continue the unconscious patterns.

ETT helps to discover the core issues and heal them. They are often only expressed as feelings, because we don't remember the underlying events. ETT' works on emotions, that is why it can help.

As we mentioned, people with a secure attachment style are able to concentrate on their present experiences and react to them. They don't filter out positive signals and they don't distort them.

Every other attachment style causes negative filtering and distortion to some extent. People who don't have a secure attachment style don't experience the present alone, but their present is influenced by their past. Their past taught them to pay attention to certain things and to neglect others.

People carry "baggage" from the past. If a present event is emotionally overwhelming, it is usually because it triggers memories from the past. With every non-secure emotional regulation style, the common question can be: "When did you feel like that earlier?" Some people have difficulties in their present life that don't need "background" healing. Nevertheless, when they feel overwhelmed, overreact, or repeat unhealthy patterns, the "baggage" has to be left in the past and its content has to be healed.

Changing attachment styles

Unhealthy ways of relating to others and managing our emotional needs can destroy our lives, but they don't have to continue. We can change. It is not easy, but possible.

As we mentioned, attachment styles are a matter of relationship dynamics. Our memories can be reevaluated when they become conscious. The connections in our brains are not static, but changing due to our experiences. Interpersonal relationships are basically attachment experiences; they can help to heal previous attachment wounds. Good relationships have an integrative influence on our brain circuits.

Children grow into healthy adults if they have someone who understands them and validates their feelings. The parent ideally should be on the same "wavelength" with the child. This is also true when we talk to someone about our problems or our feelings of happiness. We need someone who understands our feelings or "gets us." If we find this kind of person, we can enjoy our happiness more or go through our grief and pain more quickly. We are not ashamed of our shortcomings or wrongdoings. To be in comforting company helps us to be who we are.

People go to insight-oriented psychotherapy to get emotionally healed. The goal of every form of therapy basically is to help a person live a healthier life. It is intended to help a client get closer to a secure attachment style, which provides healthy self-esteem and the ability to be authentic in relationships. The client becomes able to connect and to become interdependent, but still keep their individuality. Nevertheless, this can be a very time-consuming process, and clients usually want to speed it up. With ETT we can do this.

We like to live on minimal energy. The least energy is needed when we feel stable, secure, loved, supported, and have a role and goals in life. When we have these, we don't need to expend energy to "behave," to stuff feelings, or to be overwhelmed by the difficulties of life, trusting only in ourselves.

People who have to hide their real selves, show that they are more perfect than they feel, or who are avoidant, disorganized, anxious, or deeply in denial of their needs, have lots of anxiety. They have much more tension in their lives. They need much more energy to exist.

In ETT the energy from light helps a person to get out of stuck feelings and habits, which are false and minimize energy. The light can help bring up deeply hidden wounded feelings, allowing them to be reevaluated with the help of the therapist, and transforming a person's life to live with more energy. The bad feelings can change or calm down.

The light-energy is not enough. When we have relational wounds, we need people to help the healing. We will discuss the role of the therapist in handling emotions next.

CHAPTER 6

Understanding Your Emotions

We don't realize how important emotions are. They guide our whole life. We feel them from or possibly even before birth. In old age, when our cognitive abilities decrease, we still have emotions.

People use the words "feelings" and "emotions" interchangeably. But there is a difference between them. Emotions are mainly unconscious, automatic reactions to our sensations: the reactions of our bodies to our surroundings or memories, producing hormones and neurochemicals. Our bodies' reactions can be measured. The sensations and emotions are there whether we are aware of them or not. We can react to the signals of the environment, such as danger, much faster without the delay of conscious awareness.

Emotions involve the physiological sensations and the feelings accompanying them. Feelings are the conscious realization of the emotions. Feelings are everything that our five senses can experience that we are aware of. The emotions are connected to the limbic system, and the awareness of feelings happens in the cortices.

Emotional labeling

Emotions give value to events, telling us whether they are important or not. We give more important events more attention. We talked in a previous chapter about how our brains build web-like connections between our neurons based on the experiences we go through. The frequency of the events and our emotional appraisal of them decide the strength of these connections. Our emotions decide the value of these events, so if our emotions are stronger, the connections will be stronger.

More focus on an event produces stronger network connections. The connections between the neurons are stronger if the information from an event is considered important. An important event is also more likely to be recalled in the future. A driving accident can impair the driver's ability to sit behind the steering wheel in the future. A robbery can hinder a cashier from going back to work. These are single events, but the emotional label is so strong that the person can be influenced for a long time by it.

Emotional labeling of an event happens automatically and the reaction is automatic as well. In case of feelings, the consciousness kicks in. The brain is aware of what is going on, evaluates the signals, and plans accordingly.

Emotional labeling of present experiences is deeply influenced by a person's attachment style. When someone's emotional labeling of an experience changes, the person will have different thoughts, attitudes, and feelings, as well. In Emotional Transformation Therapy (ETT) we can heal negative emotional labeling.

Emotions as information

If someone disconnects certain feelings, the planning and anticipatory mechanisms in his brain don't become activated. As a therapist, I repeatedly meet clients who were mistreated as children. They often end up with an abusive partner in adulthood. Due to the mixed messages they received as children about the abuse, they don't recognize the signs of danger, and they allow themselves to be abused again. No matter how horrible the mistreatment was, they learned to consider it as part of life and disconnect the labeling of "danger."

Alexithymia is a disorder where a person "does not feel." It occurs when the limbic center and the cortices don't work together, especially in the verbal centers. This person is "flat." He may feel something but cannot put words to it. This happens when someone was severely neglected at an early age. The person does not know what he feels. His emotions, even danger signals, didn't become conscious. He didn't learn to identify his emotions with words and thus become aware of them.

Emotions as meaning-giver

We don't realize how everything has an emotional component. I realized this after I was thinking about why I feel less at home when I talk in English instead of Hungarian. English is my second language; I have been learning it as an adult. Although I have learned lots of words, I often don't really know which word to use. Even when I use the right phrases, it often seems like something is missing.

I have always said that, for me, talking in English is a little bit like "washing my hands with gloves on." Somehow there is a barrier. I am shocked, sometimes, by how rude my English sounds when I translate it back to Hungarian. I now realize that, when I learned Hungarian as a child, I learned the words with certain emotional content and context.

I can choose my words in Hungarian with great precision. I learned the words with both my neocortex and my limbic system, which means both with my awareness and emotions. My whole brain was involved. I didn't notice this growing up, obviously.

I have been learning English with my frontal lobe, with the part of my brain that is for the so-called "higher functions." I know this language cognitively, but the emotional content didn't come through the language books.

While I have been spending time among Americans, I slowly adapt to their use of words. I sense the emotional content of the words more. Americans whose native language is English are not aware of it, but their choice of words is based on their unconscious emotional evaluation, their emotional labeling of their words.

Kenneth Dodge states, "All information processing is emotional. It means, emotion is the energy that drives, organizes, amplifies, and attenuates cognitive activity and in turn is the experience and expression of this activity." (Siegel 2012, 147)

Emotions as integrating forces

Emotions are not only inner signals of the outer world but they are integrating processes as well. They connect the different layers of understanding and functioning of the brain. They influence our thinking, what we are paying attention to, how we perceive something, and even our memory consolidation.

Emotions seem to be the main organizers in the brain. Emotions exist on both sides of the brain, right and left. Research on emotions, for example, demonstrates the intimate influence of emotions on all cognitive processes, from attention and perception to memory and moral reasoning (Siegel 2012, 239).

The integration of signals means the connection of the emotional, somatic, and cognitive information coming from an experience. The emotions help the mind to integrate signals coming from experiences and to prepare for the future. If these signals are considered pleasant or manageable, integration is possible, and the person will be flexible and able to adjust to the present situation.

Being conscious, feelings help to focus attention. They make it possible for us to adapt to our environment. This direction of attention can be very helpful in our relationships and in everyday life.

If the information coming through our senses is considered dangerous, or if it wakes up previous experiences and unpleasant memories, the integration may not happen. The cognition may be locked out. With blocked integration the person cannot react to the present and future situations in a constructive way. He reacts as he did in the past, so the person's development is hindered; he cannot adjust to a changing life. The person remains rigid. He seemingly is not able to learn from previous events.

The emotions are connecting, integrating factors between the social world and a person's inner world. With our emotions, we label certain signals of the environment as important, dangerous, or pleasant. Emotional labeling influences which cells are involved in integration, as well as how strongly the cells are involved. This self-regulation is fundamentally emotional regulation. Because emotions work as series of integrating processes in the mind, linking all layers of functioning together, they can mediate self-regulation.

This also means that emotions influence how we perceive our world at a later time. Previously I mentioned a client who is alcoholic. Although others find her attractive, talented, and pleasant most of the time, and although she is very successful in her job, gaining awards, she is sure they will fire her sooner or later. She pays attention to everything that reinforces her self-pity, her feeling of being unlovable. This self-evaluation is so painful for her that she returns to alcohol repeatedly. To stop her anxiety, she drinks. Her emotional regulation is very underdeveloped. She does not integrate into her system the positive messages of her environment.

On the other hand, one of my friends is an optimist. When she has a problem, she pulls herself out of self-pity by thinking about others who have more troubles than she does. For her, the future is full of possibilities and further successes. From her positive attitude, she gains the energy to face difficulties, evaluating them as temporary hindrances. She has great emotional regulation. She is in control of her feelings and they don't control her. She integrates both the positive and negative experiences in her memory. Labeling the negative less important and temporary, she remains flexible and adventurous. She is able to learn from her experiences.

Emotional intelligence

Everyone knows about the intelligence quotient (IQ). People are very proud when their IQ is high and don't talk about it when it is low! We regularly measure cognitive abilities with IQ. But life is more than cognition and intellectual understanding.

In his book *Emotional Intelligence: Why It Can Matter More Than IQ*, Daniel Goleman introduced another intelligence that is connected to the emotional maturity of a person (Goleman 2005). Emotional intelligence (EI) includes knowing one's emotions, managing them, motivating oneself, recognizing emotions in others, and handling relationships, which is mainly managing emotions in ourselves and in others.

Emotional intelligence is relational intelligence. It changes based on the nature of our relationships. So many of us have good IQs but have severe relationship problems or otherwise have an underdeveloped ability to stand up for ourselves or care for ourselves. High cognitive ability does not mean someone has high emotional intelligence. The good news is that emotional intelligence can grow.

Previously we talked about how important emotions are in every aspect of our life. Emotional intelligence impacts our entire life because emotions influence our whole being directly, both our brains and our bodies. Emotions impact our reasoning, thinking, and physiological regulation.

At birth our cognitive abilities are not yet developed, but we are able to feel. Due to the well-developed limbic system, our first memories are emotional. Adults often say that a child does not understand what adults do or say. This is true on the cognitive level but not true on the emotional one. Children are very intuitive. They sense what is going on. The emotional memory develops and, because it is not processed consciously, it can influence us for the rest of our lives. The memories remain intuitions, resistant to change because we don't consciously experience them.

Goleman says we think like we have two minds, the cognitive and the emotional one (Goleman 2005, 8). They usually work together in harmony.

Developmental immaturity can come from incomplete integration. Even if a person is very successful academically or in a career, when his "two brains" remain more or less separated, unhealthy emotional regulation will cause him remain emotionally immature in his personal life, with low emotional intelligence.

Emotions influence our future because our appraisal of our experiences happens with the help of our emotions. The meaning of our experiences is given by the corresponding emotions. If I consider something repulsive, I will react differently than when I think it's funny. Just think about a friend who is drunk. If I think it's disgusting, I'll want to help him stop drinking. If I think it's funny, I may drink with him.

Emotions can help us connect to each other. We can understand and feel the other person's feelings, and this brings us closer to each other. We somehow "radiate" how we feel about ourselves. If someone feels that others like to be around her, sooner or later she will be invited everywhere. When the same person becomes depressed and feels that people are better without her, even the friends disappear.

One of my clients wears baggy clothes and never puts on makeup. She acts like she would like to disappear. She was bullied and molested when she was younger, and attention brings back bad memories. But men often give her dirty notes anyway. She does not realize, despite her appearance, that she still remains a woman. The message she conveys is that she doesn't respect herself as a woman, so men don't respect her, either.

The person with low emotional intelligence can be too emotional, neglecting common sense. Everyone can tell my "baggy clothes" client that people love her, and that others try to adjust to her a lot. She still feels rejected and unloved. The sober mind is disconnected here. The negative emotions rule her.

People who like to intellectualize things don't let their feelings "speak" and help guide them. One of my clients is very intelligent and accomplished, also young and beautiful. She has a boyfriend who regularly lies to her about his "ex-girlfriend," with whom he has remained intimate. My client knows that her boyfriend calls the other woman regularly. She has followed him when he visited the other woman. My client suffers from feeling humiliated and used, but she feels she cannot end her relationship with this man. She feels she cannot live without him. This woman may have high cognitive intelligence but her emotional intelligence is low.

Other signs of low emotional intelligence are confusion about what we feel or difficulty managing feelings. People with low emotional intelligence often lack the ability to recognize the emotions of others. "Emotional communication" or empathy is the way one mind connects with another. Relationship building or maintaining for "emotionally numb" people can be very difficult. (Goleman 2005, 43).

One of my clients has a husband who is a narcissist. Although he is very charming, he doesn't have empathy toward others. He seems to be concerned about the well-being of others, but abandons them the moment they don't serve him or when they want him to change. A narcissist's emotions are very underdeveloped. The charming surface covers a shallow depth underneath.

As we mentioned earlier, when someone experiences strong emotions such as passion or danger, the emotional brain takes over. In the previous chapter about the brain, we mentioned that, while the hippocampus is involved in conscious memories, keeping the facts, the amygdala is the specialist when we talk about emotion-driven memories or actions. In dangerous or passionate situations, the amygdala can lead our actions without conscious awareness or evaluation.

How many of us have seen someone who is intelligent and functions at a high level regress and become childish in the face of danger? Movies often show bad guys who will cold-heartedly kill anyone becoming weak-kneed when a gun is pointed at their heads.

Healthy emotional regulation happens when we are able to calmly evaluate what we feel and make decisions about our reaction based on our evaluation. In this case our "two brains" are well integrated, not blocked in some unconscious circle that triggers our reaction. The cognitive part of the brain is involved in this process.

Changing Emotions

Emotions are changeable; they are not stable. Emotional intensity changes, except when dissociation occurs. Then the process of emotional change is interrupted and the emotions can stay at the same intensity.

The best way to explain this is to compare the narrative and traumatic memories we talked about in the chapter discussing the brain. In the narrative memory the hippocampus is involved. The narrative memory is changing, and the memory of the experience can be processed. The importance of the event fades away with time.

To illustrate how this works, we can think about when we've eaten a delicious dinner. We can remember the taste and smell of our food after we've eaten it. But the next day, although we remember that we had a great dinner the previous night, we usually don't feel the same joy as we did at dinner. We remember that the dinner was delicious, but the intensity of our emotions has faded.

This is not so with traumatic memory. Just ask a person who has Posttraumatic Stress Disorder (PTSD), who was injured in a severe car accident, or who was bitten by a vicious dog. The memory is not processed. It remains as we experienced it in the first place. The fear can remain the same for years. In PTSD, for example, the fear response is so strong that the amygdala hijacks the process. Every time something reminds the person of the PTSD experience, emotions with the same intensity occur (Goleman 2005, 207).

With traumatic memory, a harmless experience in the present follows the fear pathway established in the past, so the new experience, even if it is not threatening, never becomes associated with a neutral or safe meaning. The amygdala signals danger. The relearning ability is locked out. The strong emotional memory remains intact and can be triggered repeatedly. Without new associations, the fear remains.

Emotions as energy

When the parts of our brain are activated, the spider-web-like connections become active, meaning electrical energy is flowing through the web. Emotion is represented as energy flow between the temporarily connected parts of the brain that are activated by the experience. These parts of the brain fire together (Siegel 2012, 187).

As sound and light are types of energy, they can influence our moods. Thomas Mann, the famous German novelist, said long ago, "Music is politically suspicious." It changes moods.

Therapists have begun to use music to heal different emotional problems, such as conduct disorder or even PTSD. Universities now offer music therapy courses. Music is vibration; it conveys energy. The musical notes don't fly around in our brains. They are translated into energy, which can interact with the energy transferred by our neurons. Thus, music can have a huge emotional impact on us.

How about light? It conveys vibration and is energy, as well. Can it influence our moods? For years natural light has been suggested to treat seasonal affective disorder (SAD).

ETT uses the energy of the components of natural light to influence emotions, to ease distress, and enhance well-being. The light-energy can change negative emotional labeling. The light-energy interaction can increase positive emotions, which results in increasing integration. Light-energy can decrease dissociation, so the emotion becomes available for reevaluation and can decrease.

We can say that positive emotions increase integration, and negative emotions decrease integration. Integration not only increases our emotional intelligence, but it also makes life feel good (Siegel 2012, 338).

Emotions are extremely important: they decide the direction we go in life. ETT is here to help heal our emotions and our wounded lives. It is time to look at it more closely.

CHAPTER 7

Emotional Transformation Therapy (ETT)

The name of Emotional Transformation Therapy (ETT) indicates what this therapy intends to do. It transforms emotions. It can increase good feelings, increase wellness, and decrease the negative emotions that hinder us from living our lives to the fullest. In the previous chapter we saw how important emotions are in thinking, self-regulation, relationships, perceptions of present and future, and even in our word choices. If our emotions change, our whole life can change, as well.

Dr. Stephen Vazquez, PhD, who developed ETT, recognized that the psychological healing that takes place while looking at light with different energies is unique, in that it is not necessary for a client to recall certain events. Recalling the emotion is enough for psychological healing.

Consider, for example, a young man who feels his mother wanted to give him up for adoption and that nobody wanted him. Despite his mother's denial of this, his feelings of being rejected and abandonment are overwhelming and badly influence his whole life. This client could be treated with ETT. His self-torturing feelings can be stopped.

ETT uses different tools to facilitate emotional transformation. In the following chapters we discuss them in more detail. Beyond the tools that make the manipulation of different light-energy (colors) and different lighting angles, the therapist's building of rapport and ability to provide a safe haven for the client is crucial. The light and the therapist are equally important parts of ETT. They together are the healing vehicles, while the client's brain does the real work of decreasing the state of being emotionally overwhelmed and increasing healthy integration.

We will discuss the role of the therapist in the next chapter. In traditional therapy the client is healing with the help of the professional. In ETT the professional and the light's energy both help the healing. This is why ETT can be much faster than traditional methods therapists have been using for decades.

Energy of our surroundings

We don't often think about it, but we are surrounded by different types of energy that are influencing us every minute. We are in constant energy exchanges with our surroundings. Music, light, and heat impact us because our sensations and our brains work though electrical energy signals. In ETT this interaction becomes intentional and goal-oriented.

Sounds and music are vibrations that carry energy. Who does not feel differently listening to different kinds of music? Some music makes us sad; other music makes us want to dance. If different instruments are played together, beautiful music can be produced.

Light-energy also influences us. How many people have different moods on sunny days than they have on rainy days? Our mood in a dark room is very different than in a room where the sunlight is shining in through huge windows. Those who live in four-season climates know how people need sunshine after a long winter. The different components of the rainbow coming together give white light. The different colors of nature can influence us; our memory is better when we are surrounded by the green of nature.

Heat is energy, too. When we are too cold, our thinking can slow down and become "frozen." When we are too hot we can become angry easily. Just think of waiting at a red light during rush hour in a car without air conditioning in 105* heat. When we hold a warm cup in our hands, we feel warmer toward the people we are with.

If we pay attention to energy interaction, we can see how many interesting things happen. Just think about when we pour cold water into hot. The temperature becomes lukewarm, somewhere in the middle. Energy resources interacting with each other can change the outcome.

In this book we concentrate on light-energy. Our body is influenced by light—electromagnetic waves. The light enters us through our eyes and becomes electric impulse, traveling through our nerve cells. The electric impulses influence the nerve cells and through them the whole body.

We do not see only with our eyes, but with our whole being because what we see influences our whole body. The brain is built up from modules and sub-processors. Each of them is specialized to do certain tasks. They can be connected to each other or remain out of network. By looking at different colors, the light-energy can resonate and change the path of the information in our brain.

We see as different colors the different components of the natural light that have characteristic frequency or energy ranges. Because our brain transfers and keeps information electrically, it is obvious that the different colors can influence different brain functions.

People hearing that colored lights can heal often want to paint their rooms to certain colors or wear certain clothes. This is much less influential than the tools we use in ETT. In our surroundings, the paints or materials do not have clear colors, which means they have a mixture of energies. The tools of ETT were produced to have very homogenous ones. In ETT we can chose distinct colors with very precise energy. The white light can be separated into rainbow colors. The frequency of rainbow-colors.

> Red: 400-484 THz
> orange: 484-508 THz
> yellow:508-526 THz
> green: 526-606 THZ
> blue: 606-668 THz
> violet: 668-789 THz

Far red, red-orange, yellow-green, blue-green and indigo as well as magenta can be found between the traditional rainbow colors. Every color exists in a frequency ranges. With the light box we can choose target light with precise energy even within these ranges.

The different memories are kept in our brain nerve connections transporting electric impulses. These connections can be influenced with the precise energy bringing new to life or disconnect existing ones. Because ETT tools can work on distinct emotions, the healing can be goal-oriented and almost instant.

Feelings and brain activity

The more activated a brain area is, the more electrical signals are produced. Light with the right frequency can increase the activity of the targeted brain areas or calm it down.

When someone looks at the different colors, the photoreceptors convert the energy of these colors into neural impulses. The electrical impulses enter the corresponding neural circuit, which is responsible for the different emotions (Vazquez 2012b, 51).

The light-energy can have two emotional impacts. Certain colors can have a calming effect. We can say, "The color and the person who has the emotion are at the same wavelength." In this case, just like when we are on the "same wavelength" with a person, we feel understood, we feel better, we calm down. Calming down the overactivity in the brain can also cause the defense of unconscious memories to decrease and the memories to become available to healthier integration.

On the other hand, looking at light with a certain frequency can enhance disturbing feelings. When the client talks about a certain issue that causes negativity, the light can make the disturbing feelings even stronger.

The calming of disturbing feelings can happen either through directly decreasing the feelings, or bringing an event to awareness and reevaluating it. When this happens, the therapist can begin the manipulation of the ETT tools to bring up memories, in order to separate the past experiences from the present one. The manipulation can decrease the negativity, for example, while enhancing the integration of these feelings with a reevaluation of the events. During this time the unconscious can become conscious.

The right color—the correct light-energy—is important because in the brain things can be complicated. We can illustrate this with depression, which can involve four different mechanisms. Depending on the mechanisms involved, we can use different colors (frequencies) to deactivate the brain parts and decrease the depression (Vazquez 2012b, 232).

We feel distressed when we are depressed. In anhedonia, where we are unable to experience pleasure from activities usually found enjoyable, the amygdala and the medial orbital cortex are involved. In this type of depression, blue-green may help, because it resonates with these brain areas.

When something depresses us, similar past emotional memories come into our mind, so we become more and more negative. The left ventrolateral prefrontal cortex is activated. We can become aware more of the origin of these emotional memories when we look at colors in the orange range.

The inability to concentrate is one of the characteristics of depression, because the anterior cingulate gyrus loses volume when we feel hopeless. Yellow or yellow-green can help.

The color indigo can decrease the activity of the medial thalamus, decreasing hindrances to getting out of negativity. The negative perceptions can be decreased with peripheral eye stimulation.

Other colors or light frequencies can activate different parts of the brain to bring relief to other negative emotions.

Basal ganglia activation takes part in anxiety, or when someone has the desire to flee and cannot sit still (Vazquez 2012a, 225). Far-red may be the solution.

The thalamus takes part when someone feels anhedonia, when personality fragmentation occurs, or when someone is fixated on some incongruent thought and/or activities. Blue-green can be the cure for the overactive thalamus in this case.

When the prefrontal cortex is out of balance, and there is some problem with self-esteem and self-awareness, the color orange can raise our self-esteem.

The medial prefrontal cortex is involved in helplessness, hopelessness, and powerlessness. The range of yellow can influence it, changing it into empowerment.

The cingulate gyrus is mainly responsible for letting go. This part of the brain can be influenced by violet light.

We call someone codependent when she feels more responsible for the other person than for herself, and her identity depends on the other person's satisfaction with her. Her temporo-parietal junction is too active, and can be calmed down with red-orange.

In anxiety, depression, and other problems, several parts of the brain may be involved. The therapist has to identify the characteristic emotions and choose the corresponding colors.

It happens often that after one "bad" emotion is lifted, a different unpleasant feeling surfaces. This means the person's negative memories are layered, and the therapist has to help him to get relief layer by layer. The therapist has to change the light frequency or use other manipulation layer by layer. Finally, when every negative emotional component is lifted, the original depression or anxiety or other emotional problem won't cause any more suffering.

The brain areas function in an integrated, calm way, and not in partial overactivity (Vazquez 2012a, 230). When the activation calms down, new and healthier brain circuits form.

In PTSD, for example, the emotionally charged memory meets with the calming effect of the light-energy and the validation of the therapist. The past memory can begin to separate from present triggers. Current events can be associated with less dangerous emotional messages.

ETT can re-educate the emotional brain, building new associations between events and feelings. The emotional message changes during this time. "I failed my team and caused their death" can become "I did what I was able to do under the circumstances". Then the PTSD can be lifted.

After reevaluation of the past event, the client is not pulled back to the emotional baggage of the past. He becomes aware that what happens in the present if different. He can recognize what he can do and what's beyond his control.

Sometimes the new cognitive evaluation is not even necessary. The negative feeling ceases due to the light-energy.

Resource color

When I was younger, one of my friends had an impact on me like a tranquilizer. When I talked to him, no matter how frustrated I was, his calmness could bring down my angry or anxious emotions. I became peaceful within seconds in his presence.

Colors can have this kind of impact on us. Usually one color will act like a tranquilizer for a client.

Everything vibrates in nature. We don't think about it often or even notice it. Recently, people have been talking more and more about the vibration of the human body, recognizing that there are certain frequencies we resonate with. These are our resource colors. When we look at these colors, we feel good.

In a therapy session, looking at the light frequency that calms our distress is like being with another person who empathizes with us. If someone understands us, our negative feelings usually calm down. We feel validated. The memory remains, but the negativity decreases and we are able to reevaluate the event in a more balanced way. We can "see" the same thing differently. We are not stuck anymore in the overactivity that paralyzed our cognitive evaluation.

In ETT, we concentrate on an issue, feeling, or physical problem while the therapist finds this resource color. It's a great help to us. We can focus on our resource color to relax, even at home. We don't have to do time-consuming relaxation exercises; if just look our resource color, our mood changes.

There is another use of our resource color. When we have a calm feeling while we remember our issues, we can remember and superimpose this calm feeling over the issues—like superimposing our resource color over more anxiety-provoking colors. The resource color serves like a good parent, who calms down the child in the middle of a tantrum.

Unconscious

Everyone has heard about singers who can break an empty crystal glass with their singing voice. As we mentioned before, everything vibrates. The glass molecules vibrate, as well. When the singer's voice reaches the right resonant frequency and volume, the glass shatters.

This illustrates how our unconscious memories—electrical impulses through certain brain connections—can be influenced and break to the conscious surface with the help of the right light frequency and brightness.

Just because our memories are unconscious does not mean they don't exist in our brain. They are there but they are separated from our awareness. We cannot change them through regular talk therapy. We cannot reason with them. Their impact on our life is automatic. Many times we don't realize that the unconscious is influencing us.

I have had beautiful clients who have very low self-esteem and feel uncomfortable when someone praises them. It makes no sense to those who know them. What these beautiful clients don't realize is that their unconscious rules their life.

The energy of the light can bring up the origin of these automatic feelings and behaviors. We can give new understanding to past events in a way that is more realistic and much less damaging for the client in the present. In the meantime, the energy of the light helps to develop new nerve connections that are healthier.

Those who overreact to situations are usually influenced by their previous experiences that remained unfinished. ETT can bring influences from previous experiences to awareness. Learning how the past influences the present situation, we can separate them and work on them one by one.

ETT has a great advantage when working with traumatic memories. It not only brings them to the surface, but also can manipulate them very quickly. The right energy works on traumatic emotions one by one. The person won't be flooded by a sea of disturbances. They won't be retraumatized when remembering the event or events that his mind had to push out of his consciousness in order to protect him. The healing of traumatic memories can happen very quickly through the manipulation of the light-energy and the therapist's validation.

Bringing unconscious memories to the surface may mean new connections develop, which connects the memories to awareness. We will have more information about this mechanism when we are able to measure brain functions more precisely.

Somatic Problems

As we mentioned previously, emotions are mainly unconscious, automatic reactions to our sensations, while feelings are conscious. This means our feelings and physical sensations interact with each other. It is said that depression and pain, for example, have overlapping nerve circuits. Not only do our sensations influence how we feel, but our feelings can change our physical state.

That is the reason ETT can ease several physical problems. I have had several clients who were tense and anxious because they could not sleep. There was one who was so desperately sleep-deprived that she had suicidal thoughts. After working on her anxiety for three sessions, she called me to tell she was able to sleep all night. She felt much better and I "lost" a client to health, calmness, and peaceful sleep.

Dissociated memories often have somatic parts as well as narrative portions. When the forgotten experiences come into consciousness, the person can experience the otherwise numbed physical sensations. When one client who had gone through repeated sexual molestation and rape learned that she was a victim and not a valueless, dirty puppet, her body began to have sensations again.

Just like the different brain areas are impacted by different colors, our body parts need different colors to be influenced in order to heal. Because the brain is involved in the functions of our body, by looking at different light-energy, we can bring healing to the psychological origins of certain physical problems.

Physical pain or tension is usually the first thing a therapist tries to alleviate. The therapist can discover the feeling component of the physical problem and work on that, or they can use ETT, choosing colors to look at based on the location of pain.

CHAPTER 8

The Therapist's Role

ETT is not a talk therapy. Patients don't sit and talk about their problems session after session. But this way of psychotherapy still involves talking to a therapist. It is not enough to take one of the ETT tools and try to cure ourselves at home.

When someone suffers from unhealthy patterns, the origin is usually earlier narcissistic wounds. The wounds are connected to unconscious memories. The person has to feel accepted, protected, and safe to let these memories come to the surface and to be able to deal with them. If it is only a painful feeling, the client needs a safe person's company to be able to communicate it. In a way this acceptance and validation is made possible by the therapist and is enhanced by ETT. The severity of the problem is secondary.

Research shows that the most important ingredient of therapy is the rapport between the therapist and client. People can hurt us, but we also need people to heal us. Our main struggle is that we think nobody understands us. We think it is better if another person doesn't know our secrets, because he might reject us. Even the most self-assured person has insecurities.

We need another person's understanding of our difficulties.

The energy of colors can be useful but it is still not sufficient for healing. Light-energy can change our brain circuits, but we have to be able to feel another person's acceptance to be really healed. ETT is a therapy using the right light-energy of the right color together with the healing acceptance of a therapist.

There is less talking in ETT than in a traditional psychotherapy session. One of the reasons is that, with the help of the light-energy, the client can connect events, feelings, and go to the core of his problems very quickly. He won't beat around the bush but goes to the root of it. But ETT still needs rapport building and talk. Several clients of mine who were very satisfied with ETT said, "It was amazing, but the best thing was that you understood me."

People can try drugs or alcohol and they may not become a slave of the substance. Addiction is often a method to "cure" painful feelings like not fitting in. The first step in recovery is to stop using alcohol. But does it mean a person has to accept that he does not fit in? It would be unbearable. He has to find a crowd, a support group, where he feels accepted without using the addictive substance.

Feeling acceptable usually begins with the therapist. It does not mean the addiction is right. The action—the addiction—is wrong, but the person is valuable and can find others with whom he can fit in.

Influence of attachment styles

When someone goes to a therapist, the rapport building will depend on the attachment style of the client. A person's attachment style basically influences how the person relates to others, how close he lets others become, and how much he opens up to a therapist. The attachment style also influences how this person relates to himself, how secure this person is with himself, and how easy or difficult it is for him to come to and remain in therapy.

Discovering the attachment style of the client helps the therapist to tailor the way she works with him. It determines how she builds connection with him and how she helps him to address his core issues while decreasing his fear of being judged. In rapport building, the therapist must discover the client's self-defense mechanisms, what he uses to avoid unpleasant emotions and memories. The defense mechanisms are part of the attachment style.

The client has to feel accepted and safe. After then the ETT therapy tools can be very influential. A client who was sent to me had an avoidant attachment style. Everything was "hunky-dory" in her life. She complained that people found her very controlling. As we went along with the session, it became obvious that she was terrified to talk about her past or even her real situation with her children.

She said everything was good, loving, and prosperous. But it wasn't. She wasn't willing to feel or face anything that contradicted this idealistic picture even a little.

In therapy, I had to go ahead with her as she presented herself. I tried to dig a little bit into her experiences. After all, if everything was marvelous, what did we want to change? I didn't want to push her too fast, though.

Finally she let me do a little ETT. I wasn't allowed to deal with her negative feelings, though. The ETT had to enhance her good feelings. The therapy wasn't a success according to my standards, but she gained a place where she felt accepted. The ETT helped her to feel more empowered. Later she may return for more complete healing.

Another client was codependent. She was a real people pleaser. This type of client makes therapists feel good. They think they're doing a marvelous job, they're very smart—the best possible, that they've opened a whole new world for their client. But lots of times codependent clients don't gain that much from therapy. They want to be accepted so much that the change in them is not deep. Their transformation remains superficial.

Recognizing this behavior, the therapist can repeatedly check what the client has gained from the therapy and adjust the treatment accordingly. Luckily, ETT can easily guide attention to the client's core issues, and real therapy can be done.

People who have borderline tendencies, whose emotions are black and white and exaggerated in both ways, need special treatment. I tried to go slow with one client and began with her least disturbing memory. She still discontinued the therapy after few sessions. The person who suffers like her is very sensitive even to the slightest anxiety that negative memories can trigger.

ETT can help to decrease fear, but the therapist has to provide a safe place to begin the ETT therapy. The therapist has to adjust to the client. The therapist must determine when it's appropriate to introduce some new explanation, and how to reframe things that would help the client and not cause resistance.

What I want to convey with these examples is that the therapist has to learn first who the client is. How does he manage emotions, relationships, and memories? Clients have different attachment styles. Every attachment represents a different way of relating to others. That is why clients need different rapport building and treatment planning. The therapist needs to find the right way to help the client feel safe and able and willing to participate in the treatment.

It happens quite often that the client comes to therapy but doesn't really want to become vulnerable in front of the therapist or even with himself. ETT can be very good for a client, but he has to trust the therapist to gain from it. In the majority of cases, a skillful therapist can make the client feel at home, providing a safe atmosphere for the healing process with her presence and reactions.

The way a client lets the therapist build rapport can give information about the narcissistic wound the person suffered and how he now protects himself. Through feeling accepted, the healing can begin. How many times have we heard that love heals? The therapist communicates love to the client when adjusting, accepting, and validating him.

One of my favorite Hungarian poets, Attila Jozsef, wrote: "I love you because I learned to love myself through you." People often fear being judged, even by their therapist.

We suffer from negative messages and shame. If someone wants to open our eyes to how horrible we are, we'll close down and won't want to pay attention. We won't want to change. When someone conveys that we are lovable and good, we'll listen, and we'll open up to suggestions. We can consider changing.

The therapist's role is to change the mirror by which we understand ourselves and the world. We feel ashamed and insecure about ourselves due to memories that come mainly from our childhoods.

But a child understands the situation with a child's brain. As adults, we would often think totally differently about the same situation. But we don't want to remember, because the events were coupled with our self-judgment.

Fonagy suggests that the "psychological self develops through the perception of oneself in another person's mind as thinking and feeling." (Fonagy *et al.* 2003, 527-529) It is basically the same as the poet said. We need others to provide a mirror to us that makes us feel better about ourselves. The therapist is there to help us reevaluate things, showing us "another mirror."

Our problem generally is not that we are not acceptable, but that we might not dare to risk opening up to others who could prove that we are acceptable. Our wounds may have occurred long ago, but we don't dare to check whether the situation has remained the same or even whether the explanation was true in the first place.

If someone understands us, we stop feeling ashamed. We can come out of self-protective and defeating isolation. There isn't shame when we experience support and understanding.

We seek confirmation that our changed feelings are right. The therapist can be the first person to serve in this role. Therapy is a safe place. After being accepted by the therapist, the client can go out and practice new self-awareness with others.

Relationships shape our brain, the connections between neurons, and the integration between senses, time, and so on. An understanding therapist can help our brain to go toward healthy integration.

Validation

The therapist ability to give words and normalize shame-causing feelings is very important. To be in comforting company gives right to accept feelings and not hide them. This way we are not ashamed of our shortcomings or wrongdoing. Although relationships can hurt us, we need relationships to heal us.

Recovering from being emotionally stuck and having neural connections that are not integrated can happen through energy and information. Energy can come from light-energy and information can come when the therapist understands and validates. The therapist's words can help the client release the stuffed, often unconscious feelings. If the conscious is involved, the client becomes more aware of what is going on, and of the origin of his problem. Growing awareness helps integration.

The negative memories and the therapist's understanding brings new associations. The client can connect different events and see a whole new pattern form. After understanding what happened and why it happened, shame can be lifted. The therapist's attunement and validating support is essential for the client to develop the ability to soothe himself in future difficulties. With the help of the therapist, and through the therapist's reactions, the client learns self-acceptance and empathy.

Discovering the attachment style helps the therapist to tailor even her validation of the client. I had a client who became offended and wanted to leave because I said too many good things about him. He was used to feeling negatively about himself. To be praised seemed suspicious and was uncomfortable for him. I had to slow down and adjust to his pace while he developed a better view of himself.

Concentration

Another way a therapist can help a client is to increase his focus on the awareness of his problems, reactions, origin of his issues, self-protection maneuvers, and denials. If he is more aware, his brain can reevaluate his reactions and increase integration, which is healthier.

Clients often jump from one subject to another, from one feeling to another. They mix experiences of more and less importance to them. The therapist is there to help the client organize his thinking and concentrate. If the client can concentrate on one feeling at a time, ETT can change the client's negative emotional labeling, emotion by emotion.

This faster change of the synaptic connections can happen because the focused attention transports energy. The therapist helps the client focus his attention, so the therapist can shape the neuronal connection directly while she helps the client to concentrate on the problem

Choosing and manipulating the right ETT tools

My friends and clients often ask me what the meaning of the different colors is. They think that if they are sad, for example, a certain color will heal them. This is called the symptom-remedy model. They think that everyone who has the same problem will need the same color. But this is far from being true.

Every one of us is unique, with different genetic makeups, upbringings, physiological reactions, and perceptions about the same situations. Our feelings are often layered. We can begin with sadness, but it may cover feelings of anger and rejection and abandonment. We get healed from one feeling, and another bad feeling is then uncovered. The therapy ends when all of these layers are resolved.

Every person's problems have to be assessed individually. The therapist has to find the right colors that can be helpful in solving the client's issues. The therapist has to adjust the sequence and manipulation of light-energy based on the individual client's needs. The therapist can't just say, "Go home and look at white."

I learned that vividly through one of my friends who volunteers in hospitals, where she works with young coma patients and amputees. To see the suffering of people can be overwhelming. I wanted to help my friend to not absorb their pain. I sent her red-orange sunglasses, which were supposed to decrease the emotional enmeshment she felt with her patients. Putting on the glasses, her heart began to pound heavily. It became very scary. She took the glasses off. After calming down, she tried them again, with the same terrifying result. I learned that a therapist has to be present to check and adjust the impact of light-energy.

ETT is not meant to be a way to torture clients. If a client experiences strong negative feelings, the therapist changes the color, asks the client to look in another direction, or manipulates the light in a way that the uncomfortable feeling decreases or ceases to exist. The intensive bad feelings impact the person only for seconds, just long enough to recognize the nature of the problem.

The therapist's job is to choose the right tools. The light-box is powerful, but it is not always the best way to work on the client's issues. We will discuss when to use certain tools in the following chapters.

ETT therapy may last longer than two to three sessions, but it is much faster than therapy that doesn't use ETT. The client can face emotionally daunting memories with much more ease, because the right wavelength of the light gives a comforting feeling. Then the core issues and events can be discovered more quickly, and negative feelings don't block them out of awareness.

Because every session ends with calming the client's negative feelings as much as possible, the bad memories have already connected to a calming feeling, coupled with a clearer understanding of the impact of the underlying events. Often a client is flooded with uplifting feelings. The therapist can help the client to become more aware of the changes that have taken place, so the integration in the brain becomes stronger. The therapist also asks the client to write down his experiences at home, increasing the awareness of the process.

The therapist's job is to inform the client

In a way, the therapist becomes a coach during therapy. It is not unusual for a client to forget to breathe or blink during a treatment, and the therapist must remind him. She asks the client about his experience, how the different colors make him feel emotionally and physically. This helps the therapist decide how to manipulate the tools.

A client sometimes mentions discomfort only after the session. I had one client who was bothered by the light. Only later did he tell me he had felt uncomfortable. I would have made him more comfortable if I had known.

Beyond the emotional changes, physical sensations can occur. The therapist has to ask the client to share these experiences as well. ETT therapy is meant to decrease bad feelings and sensations. The method can be adjusted to the new symptoms occurring during the therapy process.

The therapist educates the client about healthy and unhealthy upbringing. A client will often say his childhood was "normal" because he didn't experience how others live. He might think he's just unlucky, and that is why his life is now a mess. But when he begins to talk about his background, a quite disturbing past might emerge. Understanding the influence of the past can increase awareness, which helps healing and integration.

It is the therapist's job to help the client put everything into perspective. Parents often hurt their children because they didn't know better, and the children remain loyal to their family. The goal of the therapy is not to destroy this loyalty, but to change the negative "messages" about the client's personality. The therapist has to find the right way to clear up misunderstandings from the client's upbringing or other relationships.

The therapist can help the client understand that bad, even unconscious, feelings don't usually change into joy in one step. The trauma model of Dr. Steven Porges (2001) states that there are at least three stages a trauma memory goes through before healing takes place. (The stages may occur during ETT as well.) An emotionally paralyzed state, for example, may change into anger first before it gives place to empowerment. The therapist has to explain this not only to the client but often to the client's relatives as well (with the client's consent).

The client is often not "cured" in one session. He can feel much better but the negativity or the unhealthy pattern can come back after a while. In this case the client needs to come back for follow-up sessions to strengthen the new brain connections. We should not forget that the unhealthy brain circuits developed and were strengthened for years. Building new ones with ETT does not require much time, but sometimes it needs a little boost.

The client decides when he wants to finish therapy. Nevertheless, the therapist can explain, as Daniel Siegel put it, "when we are loving of others, we are in an interpersonally integrated and mindful state, and when we are loving of ourselves with self-compassion and kindness, we are in an internally integrated and mindful state." (Siegel 2012, 45) This way the client can really know when the therapy is finished for him.

The client often does not recognize his progress. He can continue with his life and everyday activities as before without recognizing the healing he has gone through. The therapist can help the client to realize that his feelings and thinking and behaviors have changed. This awareness builds healthy integration in the brain.

One of my clients didn't recognize the changes in herself after ETT. She said ETT didn't help her, but she stands up for herself now. Before the treatment she didn't socialize with people and certainly wouldn't dare to confront anyone. She is still unable to react right away, but she goes back to end her frustrations and change her hurts. She also found the parallel between her present and previous experiences, so she recognizes quickly when she overreacts to something or the past kicks in. She became stronger emotionally and she dares to be angry and react assertively. She has learned new coping skills because she already understands, due to her ETT treatment, why she developed in an unhealthy way.

The therapist helps the client to exercise his free will. Until the unconscious guides him, he is not free of his past.

I can illustrate this with one of my couples. We had sessions for months, but they still had severe disagreements. I asked the wife whether she would be willing to sit in front of the light-box. Within five minutes she began to talk about her resentment toward her sister, who had always criticized the wife. She had always felt rejected, never good enough for her sister. After that she identified, right on the spot, that her feelings of rejection came from her sister and not her husband. Her husband sometimes criticized her, but it was never his intent to reject her. We had one more session. After the light-box they could talk about their hurt feelings and make compromises. This client felt and acted in a predetermined way, due to her previous experience. After the treatment she could choose how she felt about and reacted to her husband's behavior.

The therapist's job is to call to the client's attention to what the light-energy did and what results from the talk therapy. Clients often want to talk. They don't recognize that their talk changes when it is combined with ETT. They begin to talk in depth.

Skill building

The therapist can help the client to notice if there are unhealthy relationship dynamics in his present life. She coaches the client to develop an understanding of the damaging interactions. For example, she can explain that a healthy relationship involves rupture and repair. Hurt can occur, but it has to be corrected. We teach that, due to our minds being negatively biased, one negative experience should be balanced with five positive experiences. If this happens, the relationship becomes balanced again. If not, the rupture becomes more severe.

Building new coping skills is still necessary but much easier after ETT. The client has begun to feel better about himself. Now his actions have to line up with his growing self-esteem and self-awareness. The "emotionally stuck" situation is resolved, but this is only the beginning. Self-esteem builds on experiences. The therapist's guidance can help the client to develop new skills, resources, and support. The client has to learn how to care for himself, how to be assertive, and how to build new relationships.

CHAPTER 9

The Color Chart

Emotional Transformation Therapy (ETT) uses several tools, including the color chart, wands, goggles, and the light-box. Therapists usually begin ETT therapy with the color chart. It looks like a rainbow flag held horizontally. The colors are beautiful. It is a specially manufactured chart with clear and saturated colors.

When I started learning about ETT, my first surprise was that the chart is so beautiful. I looked at it and was delighted by the vivid colors.

My second surprise was during training, when I was asked to think about an issue while looking at the colors. My training partner asked me to repeat the issue while she pointed at different color bands on the chart. She asked me to close my eyes when she moved to another color.

My astonishment began with yellow. When I first looked at the chart, every color band was the same size. After I began to talk about the issue, the yellow band looked skinnier and skinnier. It didn't disappear totally, but it obviously became different to my eyes. In the meantime, the color bands under it changed, as well. On the chart, there were different shades of orange and red below the yellow. The red-orange band seemed to expand until everything under the yellow band became red-orange.

I was more than amazed. Intellectually, I knew the size of the color bands was the same and that nobody had manipulated them. Beyond that Tthe red-orange had an interesting impact on me. To my wonder, I had an emotional reaction. It made me feel like jumping for joy.

As our ETT trainers told us, "We have a relationship with colors." I knew I liked colors, but a "relationship" had never occurred to me. It was very strange and fascinating at the same time.

I know clients come to me because they have problems. I am no different. Some problems I know about and others, I don't. This chart diagnosed my issues in seconds. I was hooked on ETT right away.

This first experience with ETT had such an impact on me because more than ten years previously, I had taken a personality inventory (MMPI2) test in graduate school. The MMPI2 screens whether someone has a mental or emotional illness. I was sure I didn't, and the results confirmed this. Nevertheless, the scores indicated something quite strange to me: they were overwhelming in the anger area. I told my professor that it had to be only a temporary mood swing. I'm not an angry person. I'm usually cheerful, kind, and others like me. I don't harbor animosity toward anyone. I don't remember what my professor answered.

I had forgotten about the MMPI2 test. Then, over a decade later, the yellow color band in the chart almost disappeared in my first experience with ETT.

It turns out that, when someone disconnects from or denies a feeling, the corresponding color band in the chart appears to decrease in width. A disappearing yellow color band corresponds to when someone "stuffs" her anger so much that it doesn't even become conscious. Anger is often the result of feeling powerless, and I had been powerless during a long period in my life. It was true but I had never thought about it. Through my relationship with this color I became aware of it.

Just to make it clear, not only loud and aggressive people are angry. The movie *Anger Management* with Jack Nicholson and Adam Sandler illustrated this excellently. Anger is a healthy feeling. It tells us that something was done against us. Someone disrespected us, took our money, used us when we didn't want it, touched us when we didn't give permission, and so on.

The emotion of anger does not tell me how to react. That is my decision. We can repair our boundaries and decrease our anger with assertiveness, making clear when we don't feel something is proper. That would be the healthy way.

But many of us use two different types of unhealthy "repairs" for anger. We can become aggressive, yell, or somehow attack the "intruder." The other way is when we feel powerless in the situation and "stuff" the angry feeling. This leads to lowered self-esteem and, many times, to passive-aggressiveness. We can seem very pleasant, just like Adam Sandler was in the movie. The "stuffing" of the anger becomes a habit and becomes "normal" for us.

Just because I am a psychologist, it doesn't mean I analyze my feelings and behaviors all the time. I live most of my life based on my habits, just like everyone else. The MMPI2, and now the color chart, called my attention to the fact that I might have some issues in the area of assertiveness. When I thought it over, I realized that I had rarely or almost never stood up for myself. I shied away and often became passive-aggressive. I paid back others who weren't nice to me later on, and in a subtle way. What is this if not the sign of "stuffed," dissociated anger, which comes from feeling powerless?

And what about this overwhelming red-orange color that covered several others? A powerless person often deals with her issues as people pleaser/codependent. It turns out that people who are codependent, who pay more attention to others' feelings and stability than to their own, can be treated with this shade of orange. That could be the reason my codependency came up with the red-orange color. Actually, ETT therapists call red-orange "the codependent color."

When I heard that I realized I felt joy seeing the red-orange because I felt at home. Indeed, I was codependent then, and still am to a lesser degree. I like to serve others, pay close attention to their needs, and make them happy.

These are good things when I also take care of my own needs. But I, just like other codependents, have had problems with paying attention to or even developing my own needs, likes/dislikes, and boundaries. We want to be happy, but we are also looking for familiar feelings and situations. We often feel at home in our own mess, and I felt "at home" in codependency.

When I reported the disappearing yellow, my training partner asked me to close my eyes. Then she asked me some very strange questions: "What did you eat for breakfast? What's the color of your shoes?" She didn't seem to be interested in my answers, because she asked me two or three more totally unrelated questions. After that she told me to open my eyes.

My next surprise was that the yellow band went back to the same size as the other color bands again. Then my training partner asked strange questions with red-orange, as well, but it didn't decrease and become uniform with the other color bands so easily.

Seeing the bands go back to the real size means that my emotions and feelings were getting healed. The issue that triggered them calmed down.

After this training I can't say that I never stuff my anger or I'm not a codependent any more. But my past habit of stuffing anger became less automatic. I am more open with my negative feelings. I have begun to take care of myself much more, as well. It happened after one session in my training.

Since then I have done lots of client therapy with the color chart. Beyond the narrowing and flooding phenomena, people can see the color characteristics differently along the bands. They can see different widths at the two ends of a band, or dark patches can show up in a single band. The neighboring colors sometimes lose their sharp borders and mix together.

Seeing and Feeling

After these strange experiences I wanted to know what was happening. I learned that our emotions promptly influence what we see. Dr. Lawrence Macdonald says, "Eyes don't tell brain what to see; brain tells eyes what to look for." It can be the result of the amygdala's involvement in both our emotions and also in regulating the function of the brain areas responsible for the recognition of forms and objects (Press 2010). In general, we don't distort every color, only those that wake up emotions linked to the issues at hand.

In *Light Years Ahead: The Illustrated Guide to Full Spectrum and Colored Light in Mindbody Healing*, Liberman states that "people who have difficulties in what we call 'seeing' … have made some aspect of their life's experience 'invisible.'" (Liberman *et al.* 1996, 37) I had done this with my anger.

Dissociation means that certain aspects of an experience are not connected, or they're left out altogether. The dissociation can be seen as "freezing in place," as Thompson called it (Thompson, 2009).

If our eyes cannot turn away from something traumatizing, we dissociate emotionally. I often marvel at nurses and medical doctors. They have to treat horrifying wounds and burns. How can they remain aware of what must to be done to help the patient? Many people would break down and cry or be paralyzed by the shock of the experience. These professionals have to be able to disconnect their emotions to be able to help their patients. They had to develop a mental control, a mental shield that prevents them from breaking down emotionally.

In my case, disconnecting my anger and not paying much attention to events I was unable to change helped me to avoid being overwhelmed. It was a type of emotional regulation, a way of dealing with my life. But avoiding and not reacting to people who crossed my boundaries became habitual and later caused lots of problems. It certainly didn't help my self-esteem.

Recently when I felt out of control in an anger-provoking situation, my mind used the same limited brain circuits. I had to re-train my eyes to "open up" using the color chart. Experiencing "healthier vision," I can sense when something violates boundaries. I can stand up for myself and be assertive.

When someone neglects a feeling, his eyes guide him to a limited perception on the color chart. Eye tension can develop. Healing occurs when the person becomes able to see the colors as they are. The emotions and the vision are reconnected. The person begins to experience his feelings accurately again.

Healing

How does the healing from dissociation, flooding, or other distortions happen? One technique is art therapy. Unconscious, nonverbal experiences can find expression through creating art, allowing the therapist and the client to gain insight into the client's unconscious. The problematic issue can be processed, dealt with, and modified.

In eye movement desensitization and reprocessing (EMDR) therapy, the dissociation-repair happens differently. The right-left eye movement in the bilateral stimulation helps to bring up memories stored only in one hemisphere, protected from awareness. The eye movement helps the client to remember things and put them into a different perspective.

In ETT the colors target emotions. The emotional healing changes neural connections. When the client dissociates an emotion, the neural path won't connect to the other parts of the experience, so the corresponding color band can seem to be narrower or even disappear. On the other hand, if the client is at home with a feeling, lots of neural connections have developed over the years, and the client may perceive the color as flooding outside the color bands.

With the help of the color chart, the more neural connections can develop or the existing ones can lessen. The therapy is finished when the client is able to talk about their problematic issues and the color band remains intact.

Meditation

Those "strange" questions my therapist asked have significance. The distortion of the band is due to the past emotional experience influencing my present issues. These questions help the client remain in the present. The neural path, which automatically connects the past and present, opens up. The past influence on his vision is decoupled. When the client opens his eyes, the color appears to become more uniform or to go back to the real size and color. Emotional healing can occur. The past does not automatically distort the present any more.

The same thing is happening when one color takes over other colors. When the client closes his eyes and concentrates on the present, it helps to disconnect the automatic awakening of the familiar emotions when he opens his eyes again. He has learned to observe and be aware of his issues without the impact of his automatic emotional reactions. Now he is in the present. He can deal with his problematic issues.

Steven Vazquez mentions that ETT is similar to meditation. In meditation we try to concentrate on something neutral, such as our breathing, and let our wandering mind come back to it again and again (Vazquez 2012a 120). Although we don't try to solve any problem, our mind becomes sharper during this process. Worry and depression decrease our ability to think clearly. If we disconnect the impact of unprocessed emotional hindrances, we think more clearly. We become "smarter." We are able to let the different colors wake up our feelings and we become emotionally healthier. Because emotions inform our experiences, the freedom to feel what is going on in the present helps us live more fully.

Superimposing

Another method an ETT therapist uses with the color chart is superimposing. As we mentioned before, the brain tells the eyes what to see, so if part of the color band is intact, we can superimpose this onto the distorted part. The client can visualize the right intensity, the clarity, and the measure of the color band.

His issue distorts the band. When he visualizes superimposing the intact band onto the distorted part, this mental exercise will help to heal the emotional problem that caused the band distortion.

Our brain decides what we are looking at. But we look at things based on how our brain works. With methods such as superimposing the intact area of the band onto the distorted one, we force our brain to follow our vision and heal from partial integration.

Blanking out

It can happen that the whole color band seems to disappear when looking at it with one eye, while the other eye can see it. The disappearing band means that the person didn't collect information with both eyes. When the color band doesn't exist for one eye, only the other eye collected the information of an experience.

We don't "see" something with two eyes. Our brain collects information one eye at a time. The brain alternates between the two eyes so quickly that we don't realize this.

When the event causing negative emotions was mainly seen by only one eye, we can "blank out" a memory to totally cancel bad feelings. We can superimpose what one of the eyes "doesn't see" to the other eye. We ask the client to keep this feeling of "blanking out" in his memory while he covers the other eye. We ask him to superimpose the "blanking out" feeling onto the eye that originally saw the color band, so the person gets rid of the negative feeling that is connected to this memory.

We are still discovering much about the role of our eyes in our lives, memories, and feelings. Someday clients will be more and more aware of how we can train our own eyes to live more happily.

Best uses of the color chart

The color chart is very good if we want to assess what the client's problem is, when he dissociates, and when we want to help the person to increase his self-awareness.

Assessment

As I showed through my own example, using the color chart works very quickly to assess what a client's issues are. The chart immediately showed that I had issues with anger and powerlessness, as well as codependency.

Dissociation

Dissociated memories and events can get to the surface very easily with the color chart. Almost everyone dissociates to a certain extent. Forgetting where you put your eyeglasses or your keys—or your car in the parking lot—is an example of dissociation. In this context it doesn't mean Dissociated Personality Disorder (DID) or "split mind," which is an extreme case of dissociation. My own experience with dissociated anger showed how the color chart works with dissociation.

Self-awareness

Working with the color chart, the client can become more aware of what his issues are. He can be relieved of frustrating confusion and can feel and understand more clearly what's going on in his life.

One of my clients had never talked about his workplace problems at home. He and his wife came to me for couples therapy. His wife didn't feel that her husband loved her any more. She said he was cold and avoided her and the children.

Sitting in front of the color chart, the husband began to talk right away about his struggles in his workplace. He connected his problems to his wife's demands. He said he had needed time to prepare for an exam in order to be promoted at work, but his wife had wanted him to devote his time at home to the family.

Until this therapy session with the chart, the husband didn't think his work frustrations and marital problems were connected. He only knew he was angry with his boss, because he had had to teach his boss despite his own lower salary and position.

During the session he recognized that he was frustrated and angry not only with his boss but with his wife, as well. He felt resentment toward her for hindering him in studying for his exam. He had failed the exam and lost the opportunity to be promoted. He was bitter toward his wife because she hadn't encouraged him to try the exam again.

During the work with the chart we discovered several similar situations in his family life. The husband wanted to advance in his job or in sports, but the wife wanted more of him for herself and for the children. The husband had given up his dreams, step by step. He felt defeated by having a wife and family. He felt that the family needed repeated sacrifices from him and he didn't receive much in return.

When we discovered this using the color chart, the couples therapy changed completely and the couple was able to work toward resolution.

CHAPTER 10

Wands

Before becoming a therapist, I had never thought that eye movement was important. I paid attention to whether someone looked in my eyes or somewhere else. I noticed that I sometimes looked into the distance when I was in conversation with someone, in order to concentrate more easily on what I wanted to say. But that was all I noticed.

In eye movement desensitization (EMDR) therapy, I used alternating right and left movements of the eyes with clients. When the movement was slow, it had a calming effect. When it was fast, it helped the client to connect different events and heal traumatic memories. Recently I haven't used EMDR so much for treatment, but I often calm down anxious clients by asking them to follow the slow, alternating movements of my hand while thinking about a safe place.

In our everyday lives, our eyes don't follow an alternating path but a multidimensional path. In ETT the therapist, using wands, follows these more complex eye movements. The wands we use are each painted in a different color of the full-light spectrum. First, the therapist observes the person's eye movements. Then she follows them with the different color wands, one by one, or with a few wands kept together. The colors the therapist chooses depend on the client's words while talking about his or her problems.

This tool is especially useful when someone suffers from somatic symptoms, particularly pain in one area in his body, or fixates on certain feelings or thoughts.

We can understand why ETT works if we dig a little deeper into why our eyes move and how movement is connected to our feelings and our memories.

Saccadic movement

When we look at something, we orient our eyes to see what we want. In our brain, our attention guides the eye muscles to focus. To get a high acuity, a detailed image of something, the eye achieves saccadic movements. This consists of fast movements and stops for fixation. Our brain collects the sensory information when the eye is fixated. The saccadic movement is not arbitrary. These movements are unconscious, but guided by the person's attention (Irwin and Gordon 1998, 130). The attention guides our eyes to collect the details of an event or object during the fixation period (Mackworth and Morandi 1967, 549). The gathered information becomes part of a person's memory.

Memory development

Our senses, including our sight, collect information about our experiences. Our brain processes this sensory information and mental processes come to life (Beaulieu 2003, 521). These mental processes include memory, learning, motivation, creativity, and even our dreams.

Our memory is not of the experience alone but how the sensation happened, as well. For example, while our eyes collect information about an event, not only what our eyes see becomes memory, but the path of our eye movements becomes part of our memory, as well. The information processing happens with eye movements. The two together build the memory. These two are not only stored together, but they are connected. The different types of processing are associated with the corresponding eye movements (Beaulieu 2003, 537).

The natural eye movements that accompany thought processes are not random. They correlate with the content and pattern of those thoughts determined by the attention (Beaulieu 2003, 1671).

There is an association between eye movements and mental processes as well. When we recall certain memories, our eye movements will follow the same pattern as when our eyes first collected or processed that information. The same eye movements happen no matter how many times we repeat the recall.

There is another important characteristic of eye movements and mental processing. The thoughts and the movements of the eyes are neurologically mediated. As a consequence, if there is change in one, the other has to change, as well. From this reciprocal connection, it follows that when our eyes follow a certain movement pattern, the connected memories are retrieved. This connection is automatic and unconscious. However, we can use the eye movements to alter our thought processing.

Therapies utilizing eye movement

Both EMDR and ETT show that through eye movement the emotional content, the integrative processing of the encoded and retrieved memory, can substantially change.

In EMDR, for example, the memory cues will be paired with a right and left eye movement, which helps the reevaluation of trauma memories. Relatively newer studies of REM sleep/EMDR indicate that alternating eye movement favors cortical integration of previously disjointed traumatic memories. It helps to involve the hippocampus in the otherwise amygdala-recorded emotional memories. Since the amygdala's main function is the fear reaction—fight, fly, freeze—the hippocampus helps to involve the cognitive evaluation or reevaluation of the event. In ETT the wands, using multidimensional eye movements, work differently.

A baby's gaze

To understand the mechanism that works with wands, we'll talk a little bit about gaze. The best example is when a baby gazes into his mother's eyes. A baby's brain produces dopamine while gazing, which gives pleasurable feelings (Schore, 2012, 83). This mutual gaze can calm a baby when distressed. On the other hand, the good feeling stops and gives way to anxiety if the baby cannot turn his head away after a while. The baby becomes over-aroused, and his heart rate accelerates (Blass, E. M., Lumeng, J., & Patil, N. 2007).

Memory retrieval with wands

In ETT the client talks about one of his issues while the therapist follows his eye movements with the wands. This helps the memory retrieval because, while the client is talking, his eyes will follow his original eye movements. Following this, the memory recollection is easier.

In therapy clients want to get rid of their "stuffed" anxiety or negative feelings. If the client were able to reevaluate these anxiety-provoking situations on his own, he would not come to a session. But people are usually not able to stop negative ruminations or defeating self-talk on their own.

Dr Vazquez introduced a new idea to explain why anxiety-provoking events are not processed or reevaluated at a later time (Vazquez 2012a, 104). He states that because of the anxiety-provoking nature of the experience, the person's eye looks away too quickly from the event, so conscious awareness does not develop. Without that the conscious reevaluation is impossible.

When the therapist follows the person's eye movements with wands, the automatic avoidance cannot happen, and the dissociated experience can become conscious. Emotional and physiological symptoms can be influenced, and disturbing memories can be retrieved. The external eye activity triggers internal visual pathways that are stored together with the consolidated memories. These memories can surface and the client and therapist can process them.

We know that everything in our brain, including eye movements and thought processes, are in electrophysiological activity. The colors of the wands, representing different energies, can impact this activity. The therapist facilitates this interaction to decrease the client's distress and develop new, more balanced, integrative mental processes.

The therapist manipulates the wands, choosing more than one color or changing colors based on what the client talks about. She can turn the wands around clockwise or counterclockwise, so that the client's eyes see the color under different angles. She can change the distance of the wands to decrease the uncomfortable emotions that are surfacing. She can avoid overactivity and anxiety by the manipulation of the wands.

Our mind has an innate ability to become healthier and more balanced. The energy of a color coming from the wands can help to complete this process.

While traumatic memories consolidate in our brain in fragments, new integration can develop in a client's brain when a therapist follows eye movements with colored wands.

Best use of wands

Using wands is very useful when someone has a fixation on something. One of my clients was a child who had problem with a cousin who irritated her. The cousin, in her opinion, was too slow, too stupid, too clumsy, and so on. She had to see the cousin often, and they regularly ended up in a fight.

I tried to follow my client's eye movements with the yellow wand while she was talking about events where her cousin was "impossible." After a few minutes her obsessive complaints about the cousin stopped, and she wanted to talk about something else.

I distanced the wand gradually from her eyes, like I was pulling out her irritation, and we stopped using the wands. Because my client was a child, and her attention span wasn't long, I let her guide me to do something else in the session. I thought the technique hadn't been very helpful. But to my surprise, during the next session her mother reported that my client wasn't irritated with her cousin any more.

This client had been impatient and annoyed with several of her classmates, as well. After this one session with the wands, her stories changed. She didn't mention irritation or annoyance any more. She began to talk about how she played with her classmates. She talked about what she wants when she grows up.

Another client, an adult, could not stop ruminating on her memory of being misused by a friend. She didn't talk about the bad experience, but spent lots of time thinking about the perpetrator. She analyzed the personality of the person constantly. She could not stop her obsession with this person. With wands this fixation was taken care of. She became free of her circular thinking.

CHAPTER 11

Goggles

One of my clients was about to finish her doctoral dissertation, but she had become discouraged with how long it was taking. She was working full-time and taking her doctoral courses while raising her children. Taking the courses slowly helped her to keep up with her job and have some family life, but her motivation was fading and she doubted more and more her ability to finish her dissertation. This was preventing her from sitting down and facing this last challenge.

We tried the goggles on her. To her surprise, her self-doubt disappeared. After a few minutes, she felt energized. We talked several months later. She was happy with her new PhD. She finished her thesis quite quickly after our session. She completed her education and with it, her childhood dream to obtain the highest degree on her field.

What do goggles look like?

Goggles are black glasses that cover a person's eyes. They have small openings where the outside light can come through: one on the right eye and one on the left. Everything else appears to be black to the person wearing them. The position of the openings can be changed "around the clock."

The therapist usually asks the client to look straight while she keeps changing the position of the openings, so the client's eyes see the light in different peripheral positions through the openings. The client talks about an issue, while at every opening position he grades the intensity of his feelings about the issue.

When the client feels the zero or least-severe intensity, the therapist asks him to "absorb" this decreased or disappeared feeling connected to the issue. She then asks him to superimpose the zero or least-severe feeling onto the more severe feelings experienced with the other opening positions.

It happens sometimes that the emotion does not decrease in intensity to zero at any position. Then the therapist can put wands or sheets of different colors in front of the goggles opening to decrease the client's discomfort. When the right color is found, the superimposing of the decreased feeling to the other opening positions can begin again.

This whole thing may sound surprising, but it works. I have had clients whose pain decreased or disappeared, whose energy was boosted, whose feeling of being rejected disappeared, and whose self-esteem became better using goggles.

Why do goggles work?

We see different things when we look right or left. Our memory is different. This is also true when we look straight and let our peripheral vision work. When the light reaches our eyes from different angles, our memory and what we recall are different.

What we see with the right side of both of our eyes goes to our left hemisphere, while the left side's information is transferred to the right hemisphere. The two hemispheres store different information.

This has become obvious when surgeons have had to sever the major connections between the two hemispheres in corpus callosotomy surgery, in order to prevent a patient's seizures. Not only does the seizure activity decrease, but the personality of the patient changes as well. The patient acts like two different people.

But we don't have to look at these drastic changes. Schiffer (1977, 291) found that if someone looked to the extreme left, the characteristic feeling was usually sadness and helplessness. On the other hand, if the same person looked to the extreme right, he felt much better and in control (Beaulieu 2003, 2153).

When someone looks to the extreme right or left, information from the surroundings reaches either the left or right hemisphere—the opposite hemisphere to the extreme direction the person is looking—almost exclusively. The right hemisphere is dominant for negative emotions, and the left hemisphere is dominant for positive emotions (Hellige 2001, 56).

That means our emotions can be influenced by looking in different directions, or by the light reaching the eye in different peripheral areas. This can be used for emotional healing. Dr Vazquez explains that the peripheral eye stimulation helps the client's own inner resources to resolve psychological issues (Vazquez 2012a, 150).

We can understand the healing potential of the goggles when we keep in mind that our experiences are stored in networks in our brain. If we can connect the same issues with a less disturbing feeling, the whole memory network changes because the emotional labeling of the issues changes. The brain performs self-soothing.

While the client talks about his issue and the peripheral light reaches his eyes under different angles, other emotions can surface. Someone can feel rejected at the beginning, sad with another opening position, and so on. During the therapy all of these negative feelings should be dealt with.

One of my clients felt that she was not loved by her parents or by her partner. This feeling was overwhelming, her self-pity grew, and she drank to calm her distress. But getting drunk didn't help her to connect better with her loved ones, and they started to become unsatisfied with her and even to despise her. Using the goggles to decrease her negative feelings, she was able to find the zero-non-lovable feeling position and superimpose this pleasant feeling onto the other peripheral positions. At the end of the session, she felt differently about herself and even her posture changed. When she went home, her partner told her that a different, much more pleasant person came home.

We have to remember here that one session and one decrease of negative feelings does not mean that the therapy is finished. New synaptic connections develop in the brain when we calm our negative feelings. These connections are often not strong enough to last for a lifetime. Clients will need to come back for a follow-up sessions when the influence of the therapy lessens. Clients usually need very few additional sessions to strengthen neural connections, and each one is usually further apart in time.

Best use of goggles

As we have seen in the previous examples, goggles can be used when someone is overwhelmed by disturbing feelings, such as anxiety. If the person is flooded by emotions, goggles can decrease the stimulation. Goggles can also be used with people who are sensitive to light.

On the other hand, people can feel closed in or claustrophobic when wearing goggles. If someone experienced severe abuse in the dark, goggles can cause further anxiety. In these cases the therapist has to use another ETT tool.

Certain physical pains can go away with the help of goggles. One of my clients had both dull and sharp pain. The goggles didn't change her dull pain, but the sharp pain appeared and disappeared based on the position of the goggles openings. We found where she didn't have the sharp pain and superimposed it onto the other peripheral positions. One week later, she was still free of the sharp pain.

The peripheral stimulation of the eyes with goggles can bring up different, very important memories for processing. Using goggles can bring up unconscious memories. One of my clients who had fibromyalgia began to talk about being sexually abused when she was five years old. Setting the opening's entrance on her right side brought to her awareness that the door to her bedroom had been on the right. The door would have been the only way for her to escape, but she couldn't, and nobody had come to her aid.

I have used goggles to increase good feelings as well. One client who was extremely resistant to talking about any problems just wanted to feel good, so we used the peripheral stimulation to find a place where she felt the best and superimposed this feeling to the other locations. She felt empowered and got what she wanted.

This doesn't mean that goggles can solve all of our problems. As we have mentioned, unconscious memories or even known memories can come up and overwhelm us. One of my clients had lots of issues in her life related to grief. She usually could hide her feelings and stay strong in front her family. She was their "rock" in disasters. But with the goggles on, her emotions came up like a volcano and she sobbed uncontrollably.

Crying is good, but a therapist does not want their client to suffer for long. ETT is meant to achieve emotional awareness but not to traumatize or retraumatize a person. The goggles didn't seem to help to decrease this client's deep pain. We had to turn to wands to bring her back to manageable emotions. With wands she calmed down and stopped crying and feeling the pain. In the meantime I was pleased that the "stuffed" tears were able to break to the surface.

When I don't find a location, using goggles, where the client's negative feelings decrease to zero, I can still say I was successful if I found a location where the intensity of the feelings decreased. I often use different colored sheets or even wands to bring on the right color's calming effect, as well. With these tools I often accomplish the goal of decreasing the negative feelings' intensity drastically.

We used goggles with one client to decrease her tiredness. The feeling never decreased to zero. Her head hurt, too. Her weary feeling changed from weary to being empty while we changed the opening positions. It was not a good feeling, but less negative than being weary. A blue mat was put in front of the goggles, and her thinking changed. She was unsatisfied with herself. She found fault in whatever she did and tried to correct it, so she overworked herself. That was the reason she tired herself out. With a violet mat, her head stopped hurting. She began to talk about how interesting life could be and how many challenges were waiting for her.

With the goggles she stopped being disappointed with herself. After the treatment she began to concentrate on what to do, not what she had done wrong. She began to feel more energized.

An eighteen-year-old woman came to my session to get help with her agoraphobia. She came with her mother on the weekend, when there were no other clients in my office. She told me that she was ten or twelve when she began to have headaches and miss classes. Later she was unable to go to school at all. Now she was at home all the time watching TV and playing video games. Her parents were disappointed with her. She didn't like that, but she was still unable to leave the house. When she was young she had liked going to the beach. Now when I asked her to imagine herself sunbathing at the beach, she became panicky.

When she sat in front of the light-box, her anxiety was almost the maximum with every color. When I asked her to put on goggles, her anxiety decreased to three to four out of ten right away, but we didn't find any position where she was free of anxiety. Nevertheless, after this session, she went out with her mother to do some volunteer work. She began to remember some very disturbing events in her life and didn't want to continue therapy.

Another client had felt lonely all of her life. After using goggles decreased this feeling, I put a colored mat in front of her eyes, in the color that had brought up the most intense negative feelings with the light-box. We could decrease her feelings of loneliness even in the presence of this triggering color. She became very tired, though. Her brain had to work very hard while we did these short manipulations. At the next session, she told me that she had broken up with her boyfriend, who she knew was wrong for her. She hadn't dared to end the relationship before because of her fear of loneliness.

CHAPTER 12

The Light-Box

The most complex and powerful tool in ETT is the light-box. The client faces the light-box, a screen usually framed by dark blue sides forming a box around the screen. The therapist uses a computer to mix light-energy—red, green, and blue—in a circle on the screen to produce the whole range of visible light. With the computer it is easy to choose precise light-energy, which we see as pure color.

The goal with this tool is the same as with the others: to decrease emotional distress. Some clients want to work only on the problem at hand. If something is connected to unconscious hindrances in their life, clients often want to do a more thorough "house-cleaning."

The therapy usually begins with assessment. It can happen in front of the box or the therapist can give a short test to identify the color they need to begin the work. When the assessment happens in front of the light-box, the client repeats the same problematic issue over and over while the therapist changes the colors: far-red, red,

red-orange, orange-yellow, yellow-green, green, blue-green, blue, indigo, and violet. Some therapists use white, as well.

The client's surprise usually begins at this stage. They would never think that the strength of their emotional disturbance depends on the colors of the light spectrum that they look at.

We don't think we have a relationship with colors until we sit in front of this kind of light and think about some of our issues. Clients are amazed at how strongly their feelings change in intensity with different colors. One way to work with the colors is to assess and start with the color that is most disturbing to the client. Another way is to ask the client to talk while looking at a blue-green light. In both cases the therapist changes the light-energy based on the client's story. She uses different techniques to address the surfacing negative feelings.

Dealing with past memories

If the stored memory and the light frequency resonate, the unconscious memory can come to conscious awareness. As we mentioned earlier, if someone validates our feelings, they become more manageable. Here the therapist says accepting, comforting words while the client talks about the experience his mind had pushed to the unconscious. The repair of dissociation, the healing of this stuck feeling, can begin with this.

If the emotion is too intense, the therapist can help to disconnect the impact with present-oriented questions while the client closes his eyes. With this simple technique, the emotional intensity can decrease considerably.

The different negative feelings, such as anger, grief, sadness, fear, loneliness, and others need different colors—light-energy—in order to decrease.

During the therapy the therapist listens to what the client says and follows their words with the corresponding color. This adjustment of the light can calm the client's feelings or decrease the uncomfortable physical sensation such as headache or backache.

Different light-energies—colors—are characteristic of certain feelings or body parts. One of my clients had migraines. The indigo helped her very quickly. Nevertheless, indigo does not help all the time in cases of migraine or headache.

Another client had headaches that weren't migraines, but they still hurt. Indigo and violet didn't change her pain at the assessment. Her headache became the strongest at far-red. What a surprise! This is at the other end of the color chart. She had the most pain with far-red, red, red-orange, and with orange.

When she came to the session she complained about her husband not helping her. When she began to open up and talk more freely, it turned out she would wait until he came home, ask him to do something, but then step in and do it herself before he had a chance. She said she did this because she wanted to prove that she could do things.

Her headache came when she felt she was worthless. She wanted to hear from her husband how great she was. But because her husband was confused by her behavior and didn't praise her, she remained feeling "unworthy."

It was amazing how clearly she was able to see this pattern while looking into the light-box. After she was able to talk about these feelings, she could process them. She decided to do more to care for herself and to stop manipulating her husband to meet her needs for self-worth. The headache was lifted with far-red, the color of the life instinct, after using some eye-defocusing exercises. Violet and indigo were not necessary. Later on we worked on the origin of her feelings of worthlessness, which reached back to her early childhood.

Light-Box Manipulations

Not only concrete problems making the present uncomfortable but obsessive compulsive behaviors, addictions, complex traumas and pain problems attacking more than one part of the body, can be handled with the light-box because there are more manipulations available: wavelength, brightness, peripheral eye stimulation, the Star Conversion technique, and flickering.

Saturation or wavelength

Saturation of a color can show how much a person is aware of his feelings. Every color covers a range of wavelengths. When the color changes in saturation, we change the light-energy in this range. The higher the saturation of the same color, the higher the awareness of that feeling. One of my clients felt most comfortable when the saturation of the color was almost at the minimum. She unconsciously tried to avoid recognizing the humiliation she felt in her love relationship. After working on her rejection feelings, the higher saturation did not bother her any more. She learnt where her subservient behavior came from. She gained better self esteem during the treatment and has begun to refuse the mistreatment from her significant other.

Brightness

The brightness of a light is connected to the amount of photons and the intensity of a feeling. Brighter light can activate more and more of the same neural pathways. It can be comfortable or uncomfortable.

The reaction to the brightness of the light can be informative. Dissociation of a feeling at the light-box can be seen in the reaction of the client to the brightness of a color. If the person experiences an average brightness as too much, it usually means that the person is dissociating and trying to avoid that feeling.

Lowering the brightness usually decreases the emotional intensity. After processing the feeling, the brightness becomes manageable. The client becomes more aware of his feelings and does not "escape" from them any more. Manipulation with brightness can repair attachment wounds.

One client was a very feminine, beautiful woman. Her gentle personality didn't allow her to show anger. She was raised to be thankful and cheerful. Like every other person, she had things in her life that were irritating. She "swallowed" her anger all of her life. Her husband was unfaithful to her. When she confronted him, he criticized her for being nosy. He said she should stop being interested in whether he had other women in his life.

She was heartbroken when she came to me. The energy of the yellow color irritated her. After working together for two sessions, she changed. Originally she didn't want to leave the emotionally abusing partner. She condemned herself for suffering from his unfaithfulness. She felt powerless and confused.

After processing her feelings with the light-box, she felt more in control of her life. She began to love the yellow color. She decided to separate from her husband. After separating from her husband, he left his girlfriend, apologized to his wife, and since then he has been doing everything to gain back her love.

Peripheral eye stimulation

Like goggles, the light-box can be used for peripheral eye stimulation to change emotions or somatic symptoms. With the light-box, the person looks outs of the light circle left or right, up or down, two, four, and six inches away.

The goal is to find an eye position where the same light does not trigger the negative feeling. When this position is found, the good feeling or lack of a negative one can be superimposed on the other eye positions, which helps to build new neural connections.

It is amazing how much a feeling changes when we activate a different part of our brain with peripheral eye stimulation. The issue remains but the painful feeling or physical pain disappears.

One client had severe feelings of guilt, although she knew that she hadn't done anything wrong. After looking out of the color circle, she stopped feeling guilty after about five minutes. She superimposed this not-guilty feeling onto to the other eye positions. She left the office feeling easier within fifteen minutes.

The Star Conversion technique

Optometrists have found that traumatized people see only one part of the visual field. We can call it "tunnel vision." Someone with the "Streff Syndrome" presents this constrained visual field, even though their eyes are healthy. In traumatizing situations, our mind is not interested in unimportant details. We have to concentrate on the danger. Our eyes help us not to be overwhelmed. We develop a "tunnel " seeing only certain parts of the world.

This narrower vision is good self-protection, but it becomes disturbing when it grows into habitual behavior. We shouldn't forget that our mind is looking for patterns all the time. If something repeats, our brain accepts it as a pattern and develops a habit. On the other hand, if we see only a limited part of the experience, how can we think clearly and rationally?

After a successful trauma treatment, a person's visual field becomes much wider, and he or she can see much more (John Downing in Liberman *et al.* 1996, 141).

Using the light-box, the Star Conversion technique opens the focus of the eyes. Based on the interaction between eye movements and memory, this therapy widens the narrowed visual field and through that decreases the distressing feeling. The person begins to see the bigger picture and stops being biased to see only the negative.

One client had severe somatization problems. She was very limited in what she felt because every emotion appeared as physical symptoms in her body. We were working to alleviate pain in her back. Very soon a picture occurred to her from when she was very young. She was in a hospital to have her tonsils taken out and had been given ether. But she was still aware of what was going on and didn't understand what was happening to her. She became panicky, and fought the nurses and the doctor.

In the therapy session she was not able to talk about this scary memory, because she began to hyperventilate while crying hysterically.

When this happened, I began to direct her to do a star conversion. I asked her to look two inches outside of the circle in the light-box. I directed her to go with her eyes diagonally and around the clock a few times from 3 till 9 and after 4 till 10 and so on. I used a stern voice so she heard what I said and to bring her out of the panic. We went around the clock twice before she calmed down. While she was still sobbing, she was able to tell what had happened to her. With the star conversion her focus became wider, bringing her out of the panic and decreasing her fright drastically.

Beaulieu (2003, 3899) wrote that when we gaze in different directions, different information in our brain is triggered. For example, when we look up, visual memories are triggered. When we look down, kinesthetic memories are triggered. Gazing to either side triggers auditory memories. With the help of star conversion, we can connect the different types of memories and help memory integration. In a panic attack the brain symmetry is lost. Peripheral eye stimulation using goggles or a light-box can be very helpful in restoring it.

Flickering

The photic release technique is good for verbalizing feelings. If we put something in words, we make our frontal lobe work. Our conscious evaluation and control begins to be part of the experience.

To use the flickering technique, the therapist first determines the color that the client finds most disturbing. The client is then asked to verbalize his negative feelings while looking at the same color while it flickers. The flicker rate is slowly increased while the client talks negatively about his issue. The slower flicker rate is calming, helping the "stuffed" emotions to surface and gain verbal expression. As the therapist increases the flickering rate, it reaches a frequency where the client's conscious mind takes over. Then the client begins to feel more in control and, as a consequence, he talks about the same event with more authority. The event remains but the feeling and the thoughts about it change.

The flickering frequency influences the person's brain waves, changing them to line up with the flickering light. That is why using the slowly changing flickering can stop people who have obsessive thoughts from ruminating on the same thought over and over. Their mind comes out from the stuck brain wave position.

One client who was a military veteran had horrible feelings of guilt. He had done what any human being in war had to do. Nevertheless, certain images occurred to him regularly, and his feeling of guilt was unbearable. We used the flickering light technique with him. He loved it. He felt like the stress left his brain like steam. The flickering light in alpha wave range caused him to relax, which helped him release his horrible tension.

Speed of ETT Therapy

ETT therapy with the light-box can be very fast. One female client who was a scientist appeared to be very successful, both in her personal and professional life. But her husband called me because his wife could not sleep and was so depressed and anxious that he was afraid for her life. This woman was very tense, felt awkward in social situations, and was terribly critical of her own work.

In the second session she began to talk about her father, who was very critical of her. He had wanted a boy, not a girl, which was common in her culture. Though her mother loved her and tried to please her with her favorite food and nurturing, her mother was never able to stand up to and protect her from her father. Actually, she adored her father and was deeply hurt by his criticism.

Talking about her past while we manipulated the light, she became less and less self-critical. She loosened up. She began to sleep normally. After three sessions she called me to say that she felt good. The tension left her, she is not suicidal, and she has begun to talk to few people in her workplace socially.

Couples sessions

I use the light-box in couples therapy when we don't see progress otherwise. I worked with a very pleasant couple for months. We discussed what kind of misunderstandings they have and tried to change communication skills. We discussed what their love language was. We analyzed how they protected themselves when the other one didn't fulfill their needs for respect, connection, appreciation, or love.

They made some progress, but real change hadn't happened. The love had not returned to their marriage even after identifying and changing the unhealthy coping skills they had learned in their families of origin.

I asked the wife to sit in front of the light-box. After a few minutes she began to talk about feeling rejected almost all of her life. She mentioned how much she loved her father, who became a drug addict and turned his back on her abruptly when she was only about eight years old. Her fear of trusting a man originated in her feeling rejected by her father.

After we worked with her, the husband sat in front of the light-box. It turned out his anger at his wife was fueled by his anger toward his father, who had left him before he was born and never wanted any connection with him. After processing this feeling, the couple began to open up to each other more and their fear and anger eased.

Awareness

Using the light-box can enhance self-awareness. One client talked a lot about everyone but herself. She felt responsible for her mother, father, sister, and ex-husband. She wanted to move back to her parents' home because she felt she should take care of her mother, who was totally healthy but complained about feeling lonely. She also didn't want to date again, because she was convinced she would mess up any new relationship, as well.

My client was very critical of herself. I asked her to sit in front of a blue-green light to ground her. She began to talk about her father, who had molested her when she was young and had also been very critical of her all of her life. Her mother had never protected her. She had begun to blame herself early in life. She had been forgiving to everyone except herself.

We worked on her feeling of not measuring up. Medium-blue made her cry and violet made her burst out with heavy sobbing. Green felt comfortable and she began to feel energized.

After a few sessions she no longer felt a need to move home to her mother and give up her job and present life. She no longer felt responsible for providing her mother company. She began to have new hobbies and to socialize. She hoped a right partner would come around. At the end of the therapy she was not opposed to getting married a second time. She became aware of her own needs and values. She began to understand that not everything had been her fault.

CONCLUSION

These examples show how quickly Emotional Transformation Therapy can resolve even the most difficult emotional problems. A client told me that she had gone to a talk therapist for ten years. She liked talk therapy because she felt accepted and became more empowered to change certain things in her life. But her core problems remained hidden and she needed more therapy. After two sessions of ETT she said that, for the first time in her life, she understood why she had been unhappy all of her life and why she had experienced disastrous relationships. She felt hope for the first time in her life that her future could be different

With ETT, we can work on different levels with deep impact. We can help with everyday problems or we can discover the origin of disturbing feelings, unhealthy coping skills, and hurtful patterns in few sessions. We provide talk therapy but do more than talk. We use the eyes and the memories our eyes have collected.

The combination of the light-energy and the therapist's guidance and validation can speed up the healing process remarkably. I often witness clients who cannot believe the changes in themselves. Sometimes they are confused by the speed of the changes and they want to talk some more. I think they want to tell me: "Slow down, I'm getting well too fast!"

ACKNOWLEDGEMENTS

First of all, I have to express my gratitude to my friend and mentor Dr. Inge Guen, neuroscientist and psychologist. Without her insightful thinking and wise encouragement, this book would never have been written. Her passion to heal people and openness toward new ideas in order to help wounded warriors suffering from traumatizing events kept my enthusiasm awakened. Everybody needs a friend and mentor like her.

Emotional Transformation Therapy was introduced and developed by Dr. Steve Vazquez. His genius was to notice the huge possibilities in psychotherapy when the eyes are involved. He taught our trainers and he has been the constant developer of this method. Today he is an internationally recognized ETT therapist who has lectured all over the world. His two books are constant resources, providing a wealth of theoretical explanations and technical suggestions to every ETT therapist. He did not stop developing and perfecting this method, continually introducing more refined protocols to treat a wide variety of emotional and physical problems.

Personally I was first introduced to this method by Candice A. Ruttner-Duryea, an excellent therapist whose love for the healing profession was obvious when she invited me to talk to me about this new method for hours, showing me the impact of ETT on myself and volunteering herself to give me practice opportunities.

Jerilee Merkle and Anna Sonnenburg are our two ETT trainers here in California. They renew their knowledge repeatedly and teach therapists the newest and best ways to practice this therapy. Their humor and presentation make the training of this new and complex method enjoyable. Their enthusiasm is contagious. They have prosperous private practices, but they endure lots of tiring circumstances just to teach therapists to be able to treat clients with the most difficult emotional problems.

Last but not least, I have to thank my editor, Barbara Barr, for her devoted professional help to put my Hungarian-English into readable English form. Her meticulousness gave an easy-to-browse structure to this work. Her kind, encouraging words helped me through several difficult phases of writing.

Dr Iren Fellegvari
www.whole-person-psychotherapy.com

REFERENCES

Amen, Daniel. 1999. *Change Your Brain, Change Your Life: The Breakthrough Program for Conquering Anxiety, Depression, Obsessiveness....* New York: Random House.

Beaulieu, Daniel. 2003. *Eye Movement Integration Therapy (EMI): The Comprehensive Clinical Guide.* Williston, VT: Crown House Publishing. Kindle edition.

Blass, E. M., Lumeng,J., & Patil, N. (2007). "Influence of Mutual Gaze on Human Infant Affect. In R. Flom, K. Lee, & D. Muir (Eds.), Gaze-following: Its Development and Dignificance Mahwah, NJ: Erlbaum, 113–141.

Blass, E. M., Lumeng, J., Patil, N. 2007. "Influence of Mutual Gaze on Human Infant Affect." In R. Flom, K. Lee, and D. Muir (Eds), *Gaze-Following: Its Development and Significance.* Mahwah, NJ: Lawrence Erlbaum Associates Publishers. 113–141.

Cozolino Louis. 2010. *The Neuroscience of Psychotherapy: Healing the Social Brain (Second Edition) (Norton Series on Interpersonal Neurobiology).* New York: W. W. Norton & Company.

Feinberg, Todd. E. 2009. *From Axons to Identity: Neurological Explorations of the nature of the Self*

(Norton Series on Interpersonal Neurobiology). New York: W. W. Norton & Company.

Fields, R. Douglas PhD. 2011. *The Other Brain: The Scientific and Medical Breakthroughs That Will Heal Our Brains and Revolutionize Our Health....* New York: Simon & Schuster.

Graber, Cynthia. 2012. *Electric Shock: How Electricity Could Be The Key To Human Regeneration*. Matter: Audible Audio edition. asin:B00DNBR0KQ.

Fonagy, Peter, Gergely, Gyorgy, Jurist, Elliot, and Target, Mary (2004). *Affect Regulation, Mentalization, and the Development of the Self*. London: Karnac Books.

Goleman, Daniel. 2005. *Emotional Intelligence: Why It Can Matter More Than IQ*. New York: Bantam Books.

Hellige, Joseph B. 2001. *Hemispheric Asymmetry: What's Right and What's Left (Perspectives in Cognitive Neuroscience)*. Cambridge, MA: Harvard University Press.

Irwin, David E., and Gordon, Robert D. 1998. "Eye Movements, Attention and Trans-saccadic Memory." *Visual Cognition* 5(1-2):127-155. doi:10.1080/713756783.

Kandel, Eric R., Schwartz, James H., Jessell, Thomas M., Siegelbaum, Stephen A., Hubspeth, A. J. 2012. *Principles of Neural Science, Fifth Edition*. New York: McGraw-Hill Professional.

Leeds, Joshua. 2010. *The Power of Sound: How to Be Healthy and Productive Using Music and Sound*. Healing Arts Press: Rochester.

Leslie, Mitch. 2002. "Grow-your-own Synapses." *The Journal of Cell Biology* 156(1):11. doi:10.1083/jcb1561rr3.

Liberman, Jacob, Shealy, Norman, Downing, John, et al. 1996. *Light Years Ahead: The Illustrated Guide to Full Spectrum and Colored Light in Mindbody Healing.* Edited by Brian Breiling. Berkeley: Celestial Arts.

Lipton, Bruce H. 2005. *The Biology of Belief: Unleashing the Power of Consciousness, Matter and Miracles.* Carlsbad, CA: Hay House.

Mackworth, N. H., & Morandi, A. J. (1967). "The Gaze Selects Informative Detail within Pictures." *Perception & Psychophysics* 2:547–552.

Press, Leonard J. 2010. "Emotional Vision." *The Visionhelp Blog,* November 24. http://visionhelp.wordpress.com/2010/11/24/emotional-vision/)

Schiffer, F. (1977). "Affect changes observed in right versus left lateral visual field stimulation in psychotherapy patients:Possible physiological, psychological and therapeutic implications." *Comp. Psychiatry,* 38, 289-295.

Shlain, Tiffany. 2012. *Brain Power: From Neurons to Networks.* TED Conferences. Kindle edition.

Schore, Allan N. 2012. *The Science of the Art of Psychotherapy (Norton Series on Interpersonal Neurobiology).* New York: W. W. Norton & Company.

Siegel, Daniel J. 2012. *The Developing Mind, Second Edition: How Relationships and the Brain Interact to Shape Who We Are.* New York: The Guilford Press.

Thompson, Joy E. 2009. "Vision and Our Emotions." *Ezine @rticles*, February 28. http://ezinearticles. com/?Vision-and-Our-Emotions&id=2183902)

Vazquez, Stephen R. 2012a. *Accelerated Ecological Psychotherapy: ETT Applications for Sleep Disorders, Pain, and Addiction.* Lanham, MD: Jason Aronson Inc. ISBN 978-0765709615.

—————. 2012b. *Emotional Transformation Therapy: An Interactive Ecological Psychotherapy.* Lanham, MD: Jason Aronson Inc. ISBN 978-0765709516.